Biblical Reflections

Self Help

Biblical Reflections

Abdenal Carvalho

SUMMARY

Preface

We live in a world where, due to the hectic life we lead by various factors, we have little time to reflect on the Word of God and give greater importance to our spiritual Being, because despite being aware that it exists, we do not always give it due attention. We are not just made of matter, we have a soul and spirit that need our care, because our happiness depends upon leaving this mortal body.

In writing this work, I had as main objective to give readers the possibility to fill this gap and bring them closer to God, clarifying doubts, explaining the incomprehensible, revealing to them the mysteries of the Holy Scriptures through words that are easy to understand. I hope to be able to contribute with a deep learning for everyone who gives me the pleasure of acquiring more of this work created with a lot of dedication.

The author.

First Part

The Silence of God

On one occasion, after taking on the pastoral work of an evangelical congregation, I met a woman who brought me the complaint that she was a Christian seventy years ago, as her family had converted to the gospel when she was just three years

Old, and would never have received answers of your prayers made to God. According to his position, whenever he needed to ask the Lord for something, it was necessary for other people to intercede on his behalf. He also told me that he had already asked other pastors for explanations on the subject.

But he did not receive them satisfactorily and immediately asked him if during all those years she had walked with Christ or just with the church, because there is a huge difference between one thing and the other.

Most Christians convert to Christianity and become part of a Christian community, meet daily with brothers in the faith, fulfill their religious duties, perform the liturgies recommended by their pastors and already believe that they are well with the heavens. It turns out that things don't work that way. Before we are properly associated with religious life in the denomination where we worship the Lord.

It is necessary to be grounded in him and to live exclusively for him, through a living faith and in a holy, exclusive and without distraction with the things of this world.

To be able to bend God's ears so that he hears and answers our prayers, it is not enough to just call yourself a Christian, belong to a religious group or fulfill the commitments of our churches, it goes beyond all these things. The first step is to keep the first commandment, which says:

"You will therefore love the Lord your God with all your heart, and with all your soul, and with all your strength." **Deuteronomy 6: 5**

To walk with God is to know how to love him with all our strength, all understanding and above all things. Most Christians spread across the four corners of the earth defend a religious banner, claim to be followers of Christ and are even capable of making great sacrifices in defense of the faith they practice, but in the end they are not blessed or receive answers from heaven that they seek so much.

The reason for this is that they walk side by side with the church, but are distant from God. First of all, you love your partners, your children, your material possessions, your dreams, your personal goals, your professions and much of what surrounds you in this fleeting life, yet you leave God in the background.

The divine commandment is very clear in requiring us to love the Lord above all, in the first place, with all the strength of our hearts and all of our understanding. To love the Lord is to give up other things and dedicate ourselves exclusively to his worship.

Our thoughts, our looks, our hope and dreams must be directly directed only to him and only to him. Jesus taught us, that*: "But seek first the kingdom of God, and his righteousness, and all these things will be added to you"* **Matthew 6:33**

If we want to move God's hands in our favor, if we seek to be heard and attended to, we must first please his heart, offering him the due respect, love, consideration and adoration that he deserves. In chapter two of the book of the prophet Malachi the Lord warns us:

"The son honors the father, and the servant his master; if i am a father, where is my honor? And if I am a master, where is my fear? says the LORD Almighty to you, O priests, who despise my name. " **Malachi 1: 6**

The apostle Peter said that all of us, the church of Christ, are priests of the Most High and in truth we are, because the Word of Truth will come out of our mouths that the world needs to hear in order to be saved. The apostle's words were:

"But you are the chosen generation, the royal priesthood, the holy nation, the acquired people, that you may announce the virtues of him who called you out of darkness into his wonderful light." **1 Peter 2: 9**

As elected a "holy nation", "an exclusive priesthood of Christ" to bring the "Good News of Salvation" to sinners, we need to treat him as Father, God and Lord, paying due respect to him.

And that means putting it first in our lives, above everything else. In doing so, we will be able to cry out for your help and your mercy will reach us. John, in his first Epistle, tells us:

"And whatever we ask, we will receive from him, because we keep his commandments, and do what is pleasing to him." **1 John 3:22**

If we look to him for help, it is our duty to behave as sincere and loyal children to him, giving him due praise, glory, adoration and a complete, perfect love. Without reservations or inferior to the other things that our eyes can contemplate. There are couples who claim to be children of God, yet they love their wives or their husbands more than they love the Lord and that is a terrible mistake.

This was the great mistake made by Adam in the Garden, for having an extreme zeal for Eve chose to disobey the divine ordinances, eating with her the forbidden fruit. Faced with his behavior as a passionate and disobedient man, the Lord said to him:

"And Adam said, Because you have listened to your wife's voice, and you have eaten from the tree of which I commanded you, saying, You shall not eat of it, cursed is the land because of you; in pain you will eat it every day of your life. " **Genesis 3:17**

So, I explained to that sister that she did not have her prayers answered because she needed to correct such an error. He had spent seventy years in the company of the church, but far from God. His love, his eyes, his being, were present only in the church, in religion, in a dead faith that did not move the Lord's hands in his favor. And for the honor and glory of Christ before I left that community I was able to witness that woman witnessing divine healings, deliverances and many blessings received from God in her life.

Praise the name of Jesus always!

The Power of Faith

Numerous Christians are asking themselves why their faith is impotent in the face of the "mountains" that come their way. Jesus guarantees that they can all be removed from our lives through our determination to trust, to believe, and to pray. But why do many even make sacrifices, vows, promises and nothing happens? Did Christ deceive us in securing such spiritual victory for his disciples?

No, my readers, the Son of God never lies. The answer to that question can be found in different parts of the Bible, but I will quote just a few quotes and give you some good examples.

"And the Lord said, If you had faith like a mustard seed, you would say to this mulberry tree: Uproot yourself from here, and plant yourself in the sea and it would obey you." **Luke 17: 6**

The first condition for faith to really work in our lives is that it is more intense and true within our hearts, the bigger it shows, the more it will have an effect. But, how can it be expansive in our lives? What does it really mean to "increase faith"? Our faith grows with each success achieved in our journey as Christians and dependents of God in this world. Those who usually receive the answers to their prayers and are commonly blessed start to trust the Lord more, as there will be no doubt in their minds when they call upon Him for certain things.

The Christian who prays, cries out, asks and receives nothing from God will end up becoming an unbeliever and loses the courage to insist on his supplications. Thus, it is extremely necessary that in order to increase our faith it is necessary to live a new experience with our Lord each day.

But, how can those who pray and are not answered grow their faith? Well, for these they must first correct this serious problem, understanding the reason why the sky is behind closed doors for them.

Several reasons can lead God to not want to hear our prayers or answer our pleas, the most common of which is sin. In chapter five of the book of the prophet Jeremiah, we read:

"Your iniquities turn away from these things, and your sins separate good from you." Jeremiah 5:25

Isaiah warned:

"But your iniquities are separating you from your God; and your sins cover his face from you, lest he hear you. "

Isaiah 59: 2

João, too, gave his warning:

"Anyone who is born of God does not commit sin; because its seed remains in it; and he cannot sin, because he is born of God. "

1 John 3: 9

Therefore, we see that one of the main causes of God's silence is the practice of sin on a voluntary basis, that is, when one sins of his own free will and not because of the natural weakness of human flesh.

An example of this is our constant idolatry for the things of this world, like the love of money. Materialistic people displease the Holy Spirit and he withdraws from their lives, as the Scriptures warn us about such sin:

"Because the love of money is the root of all kinds of evils; and in that greed some have strayed from the faith, and pierced themselves with many pains." 1 Timothy 6:10

"No one can serve two masters; because he will either hate the one and love the other, or he will devote himself to one and despise the other. You cannot serve God and money." Matthew 6:24

This is just one of many other voluntary sins that man, both Christian and atheist, can commit deliberately. Materialism is idolatry and as such it ignites the wrath of God against those who practice it. During my pastoral life I have seen many brothers whose love of money is extreme, especially other religious leaders who have already been dominated by this passion to the point of having turned their ministries into a business, seeking only material profits rather than worrying about salvation. of souls who are still lost and imprisoned in sin.

The practice of idolatry is directly linked to attachment to everything that exists in this world, both to material goods and to people, desires for conquest, dreams, ideas and even the ministry that we may exercise.

God is too zealous for his own honor and does not allow it to be exchanged for anything else. If we want to continue to be blessed, it is necessary to put Him first in our hearts or do nothing. Through Isaiah's mouth, he warned:

"I am the Lord; this is my name; I will not give my glory to others, nor my praise to the images of sculpture." Isaiah 42: 8

A son who does not honor his father has no merit before him, so how can he want to receive anything? The same is true in the relationship between Christ and his church. If we do not give him due worship, honor, glory and praise, how do we still want to receive from him the blessings we ask for through our prayers? Let us think about it and strive to correct our faults so that we can reach mercy.

Another thing we must consider about an impotent faith that makes it happen in our lives is the fact that it needs to be alive and effective. A faith that is not accompanied by good works is dead and does nothing, as the apostle James tells us:

"My brothers, what good is it if someone says they have faith and do not have works? Can faith save you? And if your brother or sister is naked, and they lack daily food,

And any of you say to them: Go in peace, warm up and be satisfied; and you don't give them the necessary things for the body, what benefit will there be? So also faith, if it does not have works, is dead in itself. But someone will say: You have faith, and I have works; show me your faith without your works, and I will show you my faith by my works.

You believe that there is only one God; you do well. The demons also belive and tremble. But, O vain man, do you want to know that faith without works is dead. Was not our father Abraham justified by works, when he offered his son Isaac on the altar?

You see that faith cooperated with his works, and that through works faith was perfected. And the Scripture was fulfilled, which says:

And Abraham believed God, and it was counted as righteousness, and he was called the friend of God. You see then that man is justified by works, and not just by faith. And was not Rahab, the harlot, also justified by the works, when she collected the emissaries, and dismissed them in another way? For just as the body without the spirit is dead, so also faith without works is dead. **James 2: 14-26**

Therefore, we see in this biblical text that we need to unite our faith with the practice of good works or otherwise it will become dead, that is, totally insignificant in our lives. Many Christians show a great deal of faith in God and his promises, but they do nothing for their fellowmen.

Whole churches live day and night in prayer and achieve nothing, as they are inert before hundreds of people — saved or not — who are starving, naked, sick, homeless, injustice and need divine intervention in their lives and it is our duty to help- materially and intercede for the salvation of Christ to reach them.

To be prostrate crying out to God only for ourselves and our families without taking into account the basic needs of our neighbors who may need our help is Christian hypocrisy, as it is the duty of every human being to reach out to those who cry out.

The Lord is just and will not extend his hand in favor of those who refuse to help those most in need, as he himself said that 'it is by giving that one receives". Our God is concerned about our needs and wants us to do the same for our fellow men.

Moses warned the Israelites of this particular character of the Most High, when he said:

"For the LORD your God is the God of gods, and the Lord of lords, the great, mighty and terrible God, who is no respecter of persons, nor accepts rewards. Who does justice to the orphan and the widow, and loves the foreigner, giving him bread and clothes. " **Deuteronomy 10: 17,18**

Jesus said:

"Therefore, whatever you want men to do to you, do to them also, because this is the law and the prophets." **Matthew 7:12**

If we want to receive the good of God, then let us do the same good to our neighbor regardless of whether he is a Christian like us or not. The biggest mistake of modern religions is to claim that their members should show mercy only to those who share the same faith, however that is not what the Scriptures teach. Christ said:

"But I say to you, love your enemies, bless those who curse you, do good to those who hate you, and pray for those who mistreat you and persecute you; that you may be children of your Father who is in heaven;

Because it causes your sun to rise on the bad and the good, and the rain to descend on the just and the unjust. For if you love those who love you, what reward will you have?

Don't the tax collectors do the same? And if you only greet your brothers, what do you do too much?

Don't the tax collectors do that too? Be ye therefore perfect, as your Father in heaven is perfect."

Matthew 5: 44-48

Divisions of Faith

Faith is divided into three distinct phases and in order for it to work correctly, it must be carried out by its owner. Let's see below each one of them and their particularities:

1- Believing that God really exists and is capable of accomplishing the impossible — The first thing that the human being must do so that everything he wants to be able to materialize in his life is to believe in the person of Christ, accept him as the only Savior and hand over his ways, because the Scriptures warn: *"your way to the Lord; trust him, and he will do everything. "* **Psalm 37: 5**

This makes us understand that after meeting him and accepting him as Lord, we must first give him our ways, that is, our dreams and projects so that they can be confirmed by him and trust that he loves us and wishes to bless us, after all, he gave the life of his only son to rescue us from eternal death and will not refuse to bless us with what we need. Remember what Jesus told us:

"He who asks, receives; and, what seeks, finds; and to the beat it will open. And who among you is the man who, asking his son for bread, will give him a stone? And, asking for fish, will he give you a snake? If you then, being evil, know how to give good things to your children, how much more will your Father in heaven give goods to those who ask him? " **Matthew 7: 8-11**

Doubting God's immense mercy and his willingness to bless us after he gave us the life of an only child is an affront to us.

2 - Believing that he is the God of the impossible. — The second phase of faith is not to doubt its infinite capacity to accomplish all things. We often sin by letting a root of doubts lead us to ask inwardly whether the Lord will really be able to accomplish certain things for us, both because of our lack of merit and because of the size of the obstacles to be faced in order to determine goal is achieved.

First, we sin because we want to limit the Lord's realizing power to our powerlessness as human beings, we forget that no giant is so big that it prevents God's action on our behalf.

Second, we sin by imagining God as a being like us, bound to live in this world and not living in the heavens and his infinite realizing force expands in the horizontal and vertical directions, from top to bottom, above the earth and even his most deep chasms. Winds, storms, fire, rain and all nature obey him. Our God is great in glory, strength, holiness and power. Nothing can stop your action. In Isaiah, we read:

"Even before there was a day, I am; and there is none that can escape my hands; I acting, who will stop him?" **Isaiah 43:13**

Who can prevent God's action in our lives? So let us do as the prophet did, who said:

"Even though the fig tree does not bloom, nor is there any fruit in the vine; even though the olive product is disappointing, and the fields do not produce food; even though the spotted sheep are snatched, and there are no cattle in the corrals; Yet I will rejoice in the Lord; I will rejoice in the God of my salvation." **Habakkuk 3: 17,18**

3 - To confidently await our victory in Christ — The third phase of living and effective faith is the disposition that man, now saved and cleansed from his sins, must have in believing that his victory in Christ is certain. Just as the union between darkness and light is not possible, so communion between faith and doubt becomes impossible, because in the same way that light dispels darkness, doubt weakens trust.

Whoever gets used to doubting everything in life will hardly receive anything from God, because the writer of the letter to the Hebrews warns us:

"Now, without faith, it is impossible to please him; because it is necessary that those who approach God believe that he exists, and that he is a rewarder of those who seek him." **Hebrews 11: 6**

Doubt is a spiritual poison against faith, for it not only limits its power, but also prevents our pleas from reaching the ears of the Most High and moving his hands in our favor. The Lord abhors doubtful man because he distrusts his infinite power, his infinite capacity to accomplish all things and that he is seated on his throne above the earth, in the Universe, having total control over everything and everything.

It is not enough to just accept Christ, convert to Christianity, belong to an evangelical denomination, defend the flag of this or that church, but have a living and effective faith in the Almighty Holy One of Israel. Now I invite you, beloved reader, to answer the following questions to yourself:

a) What is keeping you from being blessed by God?

b) Is your faith being true and effective?

c) Are you putting the three phases of faith into practice?

4) How is your relationship with God, do you really love him above all else, or is your heart distracted by the things of this world?

5) Have you really walked with Christ or just with the Church?

Don't Love the World

One day a young man belonging to the Christian congregation where I pastored called me aside, after the end of a service, and asked me about the topic addressed in the sermon I preached during Sunday School that Sunday morning. Our conversation took place as I will show below:

— Pastor, what does it really mean "not to love the world ...?"

— First, let's understand what João wanted to explain to us, by saying:

"Do not love the world or what is in the world. If anyone loves the world, the Father's love is not in it." 1 John 2:15

To love the world is to fervently desire everything it can offer us. For example: Worldly diversions, vanities, carnal desires, drugs, materialism that ends up becoming a form of idolatry, all kinds of addictions and religious modernism that supports and defends sexual immorality, such as homosexuality and sex free in the lives of young people, inside and outside the churches.

"Not to love the world", therefore, is never to want to practice all your lusts and not to support such things in any way, but to severely condemn them as sin and affront God. Many who call themselves Christians today go hand in hand with the new moderns. Certain religious ideas created by the corrupt minds of pastors interested only in crowding their luxurious temples of tithe payers and offerers. They only appreciate having a corral full of goats that rejoice in having the freedom to live deliberately. Practicing all kinds of sin, hiding their iniquities behind a false appearance of Christians, but that at the end of the month fill the temple treasury with money.

And care little for the true sheep who remain faithful to the Lord, cherishing holiness, rejecting worldliness, but who are so poor that their contributions do not even pay for the congregation's expenses.

About these pastors of iniquity, the Scriptures warn us:

"And the word of the LORD came to me, saying,

Son of man, prophesy against the shepherds of Israel; prophesy, and say to the shepherds: Thus says the Lord GOD: Woe to the shepherds of Israel who feed themselves! Should not shepherds feed the sheep?

You eat fat, and you put on wool; kill the barley; but do not feed the sheep. The weak have not strengthened, and the sick have not healed, and the broken have not called, and the stray have not brought back, and the lost have not sought; but you dominate them with rigor and harshness.

So they spread, because there was no shepherd, and became pasture for all the beasts of the field, because they spread. My sheep went astray in all the mountains, and in all the high hill; yea, my sheep have been scattered all over the face of the earth.

There was no one to ask for them, nor anyone to look for them. Therefore, shepherds, I have heard the word of the Lord: I live, says the Lord GOD, who, because my sheep have been given over to prey. And my sheep came to be used as pasture for all the beasts of the field, for want of a shepherd, and my shepherds did not seek out my sheep; and the shepherds fed themselves, and they did not feed my sheep. Therefore, O shepherds, hear the word of the Lord: Thus says the Lord GOD: Behold, I am against shepherds; I will demand my sheep from their hands, and they will no longer feed the sheep.

Pastors will no longer feed themselves; and I will save my sheep from their mouth, and they will no longer be pasture. For thus says the Lord GOD: Behold, I, myself, will search for my sheep, and will seek them out.

As the shepherd seeks his flock on the day when he is in the midst of his scattered sheep, so will I seek my sheep; and I will free them from all the places where they are scattered, in the cloudy and dark day. And I will take them out of the peoples, and gather them from the countries, and bring them to their own land, and I will feed them in the mountains of Israel, by the rivers, and in every dwelling on earth.

I will feed them in good pastures, and in the high mountains of Israel it will be their fold; there they will lie down in a good fold, and will graze in fat pasture in the mountains of Israel. I myself will feed my sheep, and I will make them rest, says the Lord GOD. I will seek the lost, and the stray I will bring again, and the broken will call, and the sick will strengthen; but the fat and the strong I will destroy; I will feed them with judgment." **Ezekiel 34: 1-16**

Love or permanent fellowship with the modern world has led many of those who were truly saved in the person of Christ Jesus to return to their former state of sin. And, therefore, destitute they returned to the grace of God, their current spiritual state getting worse than before, when they did not yet know their salvation. Judas, brother of the Lord, advises us:

"But I want to remind you, as I already knew this, that, when the Lord saved a people, taking them out of the land of Egypt, he then destroyed those who did not believe. And to the angels who did not keep their principality, but left their own habitation.

27

He reserved in darkness and in eternal prisons until the judgment of that great day. As well as Sodom and Gomorrah, and the surrounding cities, who, having given themselves up to fornication like those, and gone after another flesh, were put, for example, suffering the penalty of eternal fire.

And yet, these too, similarly asleep, contaminate their flesh, and reject domination, and vituperate dignities.

But Archangel Michael, when he contended with the devil, and disputed over the body of Moses, did not dare to pronounce a curse judgment against him; but he said, The Lord rebuke you.

These, however, speak ill of what they do not know; and, in what they naturally know, how irrational animals become corrupted.

Woe to them! because they entered the path of Cain, and were taken in by the mistake of Balaam's prize, and perished in the contradiction of Korah.

These are stains in your love parties, feasting with you, and feeding themselves without fear.

They are clouds without water, carried by winds from one place to another; they are like withered, fruitless trees, twice dead, uprooted. Fiery waves of the sea, which skim their very abominations; wandering stars, for whom the blackness of darkness is forever reserved. And of these Enoch, the seventh after Adam, also prophesied, saying,

Behold, the Lord is coming with thousands of his saints. To judge against all and to condemn all the wicked among them, for all their wicked works that they wickedly committed, and for all the harsh words that wicked sinners spoke against him.

These are mumblers, complainers of their luck, walking according to their lusts, and whose mouth says very arrogant things, admiring people because of interest.

But you, beloved, remember the words that were foretold to you by the apostles of our Lord Jesus Christ. Who told you that in recent times there would be scoffers who would walk according to their wicked lusts.

These are the ones who separate themselves, sensual, who do not have the Spirit. But you, beloved ones, building yourselves up on your most holy faith, praying in the Holy Spirit.

Keep yourselves in the love of God, waiting for the mercy of our Lord Jesus Christ for eternal life. And have pity on some, using discernment. And save some with fear, snatching them from the fire, hating even the flesh-stained tunic.

Now to him who is able to keep you from stumbling, and to present you blameless, with joy, before his glory,

To the only wise God, our Savior, be glory and majesty, dominion and power, now, and forever. Amen." **Jude 1: 5-25**

Paul, writing his letter to the brothers residing in the church founded in Galatia, detailed the characteristics of those who live in the flesh and not in the spirit, both those who are still without Christ and those who, even after being reached by His Grace, have become trapped in worldliness.

"Because the works of the flesh are manifest, which are: adultery, fornication, impurity, lust, Idolatry, witchcraft, enmities, porfias, emulations, wraths, fights, dissensions, heresies, Envies, homicides.

Drunkenness, gluttonies, and the like to these, about whom I declare to you, as I told you before, that those who commit such things will not inherit the kingdom of God. But the fruit of the Spirit is: love, joy, peace, patience, kindness, kindness, faith, meekness, temperance." Galatians 5: 19-22

In this way, dear young man, we understand through the Word of God that "to love the world" is to insistently want to participate in his lusts and to want to feed on the sin-poisoned lentils that he offers us in order to distance ourselves from the living God.

— I understand, Pastor

And so we end our dialogue. That boy finally understood the importance of staying away from worldliness and avoiding at all costs being contaminated with the mistakes that Satan has planted in the church's mind.

The Holiness of the Christian According to the Bible

A large number of Christians, especially the youngest, question the true meaning of the term "holiness" found in Hebrews 12:14. In fact, being holy before God's eyes has nothing to do with human perfection, as this will never happen as long as we live in this world.

The sanctity required by God of man is related to a new way of living in the midst of a world corrupted and full of immoralities, a condition that makes the human soul remain dead in crimes and sins, because the term "death" here corresponds to a state of separation between God and his rebellious creatures since the fall of our first parents in Eden.

Paul clarified to the Corinthians that:

"Because just as death came for a man, so also the resurrection of the dead came for a man. Because just as everyone dies in Adam, so will everyone be quickened in Christ." 1 Corinthians 15: 21,22

When the sinner is converted to Christ, he is cleansed of all his sins and his soul becomes white as snow, completely cleansed from sin. However, if he commits new crimes, because of his inclination to evil, he will once again be a slave to Satan.

And in this way he will lose the bond of communion with the Lord. So, so that this old condition can be redone and its name can be found in the Lamb's Book of Life, it is necessary to seek again the sanctity of body and soul now again in the mud of sins. Paul, in his letter to the Ephesians, rebukes them:

"And I say this, and I testify in the Lord, that you will no longer walk as other Gentiles do, in the vanity of their mind.

Blackened in understanding, separated from the life of God by the ignorance in them, by the hardness of their hearts.

Who, having lost all feeling, surrendered themselves to dissolution, so as to greedily commit all impurity. But you did not learn Christ that way. If you have heard it, and been taught in it, how is the truth in Jesus?

That, as for the past dealings, dispose of the old man, who is corrupted by the lusts of deception. And renew yourself in the spirit of your mind.

And put on the new man, who according to God is created in true justice and holiness. Therefore, leave the lie, and speak the truth each with your neighbor; because we are members of each other.

Be angry, and do not sin; do not let the sun go down on your anger.

Give no place to the devil. He who stole, don't steal anymore; rather work, doing with your hands what is good, so that you have something to share with what you need. No nasty words will come out of your mouth, but only the one that is good for promoting edification, so that it will give grace to those who hear it. And do not grieve the Holy Spirit of God, in whom you are sealed for the day of redemption. All bitterness and anger and anger and shouting and blasphemy and all malice are taken away from you.

Rather be kind and merciful to one another, forgiving one another, just as God forgave you in Christ." **Ephesians 4: 17-32**

The apostle's advice to that church is to stay away from evil and avoid returning to the old worldly habits, where you lived dissolute and without any fear of God. This new posture recommended to the brothers of that time clearly shows us the correct way in which all of us, disciples of Christ, must behave before him and the world so that we are not subject to scandals or come to lose our communion with God and the guarantee of salvation received through the faith that we once had in him who shed his blood for us on the Cross of Calvary.

To the brothers in Thessalonica, Paul warned:

"Because God did not call us for filth, but for sanctification." **1 Thessalonians 4: 7**

"May each of you know how to possess your vessel in sanctification and honor."

1 Thessalonians 4: 4

"For this is the will of God, your sanctification; to abstain from fornication. **"1 Thessalonians 4: 3**

To the Hebrews, he concludes:

"Follow peace with all, and sanctification, without which no one will see the Lord." **Hebrews 12:14**

To the Romans:

"But now, freed from sin, and made servants of God.

You have your fruit for sanctification, and ultimately, eternal life." Romans 6:22

"I speak as a man, because of the weakness of your flesh; for as you have presented your members to serve uncleanness and wickedness to wickedness, so now present your members to serve justice for sanctification." Romans 6:19

To the Corinthians:

"Now, beloved, since we have such promises, let us cleanse ourselves of all filthiness of the flesh and spirit, perfecting sanctification in the fear of God." 2 Corinthians 7: 1

Thus, there are countless recommendations in the Holy Scriptures for all of us Christians to seek to depart from sin and association with the modern world, because our friendship with him represents enmity with God. So, be prudent, be alert, for the coming of Christ is near to take your church, the one truly washed and bought in your blood, formed by sincere Christians in your faith, pure and sanctified in all ways of living, totally separated for your worship.

Today's False Prophets

O ur temples are filled with false prophets who, like ancient times, tried to deceive the people of God with their deceitful revelations and distorted views by Satan. And the recommendation that was given by God in the past through the mouth of his true representatives still remains valid, since the Holy Spirit warns us of the arrival of these children of the evil one in our midst.

Through Jeremiah's mouth, he warned:

"For thus says the Lord of hosts, the God of Israel: Do not let your prophets in the midst of you, your diviners, or listen to your dreams, which you dream deceive you." **Jeremiah 29: 8**

"And the Lord said to me, The prophets prophesy falsely in my name; I never sent them, nor gave them orders, nor spoke to them; false vision, and divination, and vanity, and the deceit of your heart is what they prophesy to you." **Jeremiah 14:14**

"Because I did not send them, says the Lord, and they prophesy falsely in my name; so that I cast you out and perish, you and the prophets who prophesy to you." **Jeremiah 27:15**

"Prophets prophesy falsely, and priests rule by their hands, and my people so desire; but what will you do at the end of this? " **Jeremiah 5:31**

Through Moses:

"You will not hear the words of that prophet or dream dreamer; because the Lord your God is testing you. To know whether you love the Lord your God with all your heart, and with all your soul." Deuteronomy 13: 3

"And that prophet or dreamer of dreams will die, because he spoke rebellion against the Lord your God, who brought you out of the land of Egypt, and rescued you from the house of bondage, to separate you from the way that the Lord your God commanded you to walk. in him: thus you will remove evil from among you. " Deuteronomy 13: 5

Christ warned his disciples:

"Because false Christs and false prophets will arise, and will do such great signs and wonders that, if possible outside, they would deceive even the chosen ones." Matthew 24:24

"Beware, however, of false prophets, who come to you dressed as sheep, but inwardly they are devouring wolves." Matthew 7:15

Through Pedro:

"And there were also false prophets among the people, just as among you there will also be false doctors, who will covertly introduce heresies of perdition, and will deny the Lord who redeemed them, bringing upon themselves sudden perdition." 2 Peter 2: 1

By João: *"Beloved, do not believe with all your spirit. Rather, test whether the spirits are of God, because many false prophets have already risen in the world.* 1 John 4: 1

There are still those who believe in the erroneous idea that it is necessary to go looking for "prophets" so that they can intercede with God so that he can answer their prayers as they did in Old Testament times, but this is a tremendous mistake.

Since Christ was given on the cross as a living sacrifice for our sins, that need has been abolished, for he is now our Eternal High Priest. When Jesus was resurrected, he returned to heaven and sat there at the right hand of the Father, Almighty, and there he intercedes for each one of us, his church, and therefore, human intercessors are no longer necessary, as the biblical text found in the letter explains. to the Hebrews:

"And, in fact, those were made priests in large numbers, because by death they were prevented from remaining. But this one, because it remains forever, has a perpetual priesthood.

Therefore, he can also perfectly save those who come to God through him, always living to intercede for them.

Because such a high priest suited us, holy, innocent, spotless, separated from sinners, and made more sublime than the heavens.

That he did not need, like the high priests, to offer sacrifices every day, first for his own sins, and then for the people. Because this he did, once, offering himself. Because the law constitutes high priests to weak men, but the word of the oath, which came after the law, constitutes the Son, perfect forever. Hebrews 7: 23-28

If we have a High Priest in heaven who lives eternally, interceding day and night for us, why would we ask for help from a failed human being?

Imperfect and prone to commit the same faults as we did to ask in our favor before God's throne? These heretics place themselves in the middle of the church, claiming to be emissaries of God and exploiting the most unwary in the faith and ignorant of the Word of God to take advantage of their ignorance. Most sell outright divine gifts, whether or not these individuals exist, and even those who exchange their prophetic services for food baskets or other forms of financial support.

But, as the Lord said through Jeremiah, the prophets who rise up in the middle of the church were not always actually sent by him, nor did he command any prophecy to be uttered before his people. Therefore, do not be deceived, as the apostle said, let us test the spirits to see if they really belong to God.

The Time

Nothing can put all things in their place other than "time". It heals wounds, erases bad memories, corrects injustices, straightens what is crooked, closes distances, clears doubts, turns enemies into friends, darkness into light, death into life, sadness into joy, hate into love, grudges into forgiveness, storm in calm. The writer of Ecclesiastes thus describes the performance of time:

"For everything there is an occasion, and a time for each purpose under heaven, a time to be born and a time to die, a time to plant and a time to uproot what has been planted.

Time to kill and time to heal, time to tear down and time to build, time to cry and time to laugh, time to mourn and time to dance, time to spread stones and time to gather them, time to embrace and time to restrain yourself.

Time to look and time to give up, time to keep and time to throw away, time to rip and time to sew, time to shut up and time to talk, time to love and time to hate, time to fight and time to live in peace. " **Ecclesiastes 3: 1-8**

Sometimes we get upset because what we ask of the Lord takes time to materialize in our lives, forgetting that everything happens in God's time and not in ours. The Bible teaches us that a day for him is like a thousand years and a thousand years as a day.

That is, what seems to us to be an eternity for him is just a moment. Rush is the enemy of time, it brings us agony, impatience, despair, hopelessness, restlessness, nervousness and lack of peace. However, if we have the wisdom to wait for time to act, it will lead us to our goal at the right time and we will certainly be successful. One of the most powerful Eastern doctrines is meditation, as it leads those who practice it to achieve the gift of patience. Patient individuals are more likely to achieve victory in their purposes because they know how to wait.

As Solomon said, there is time for everything under heaven. This is the great secret of the true winners, the patience to wait for the exact moment to take the first step towards their goals. God is infinitely powerful to build the earth and the entire universe in a second, but as it is written in Genesis he did it all in seven days. To be patient is to know how to wait for time, to let him do everything in his own way.

A few days ago we lost a loved one in our family and when I saw his wife and daughter in complete despair I tried to comfort them, even though it seemed to be rude and rude, telling them that it was a natural part of the life of every human being . The deceased was my blood brother, the eldest, whose age was over sixty. Of course it hurts immensely to lose a father, husband and brother, but after we shed a few tears in farewell, we need to move on.

Since we grew up and started to understand life, we have already understood that one day our time of existence in this world is limited and no one, whether rich or poor, escapes one day to make that journey to the other side. We can even neglect this truth, pretend we don't care, we don't care, but that day will come for everyone, regardless of who it is.

Millionaires and powerful people may even have the power to make their stays here on earth longer, exchange a defective organ, replace a heart, a liver, properly treat an incurable disease and thus survive with it for decades, but at the end of all your efforts will come time to leave, because there is no way, death is certain. It is a natural process, no one will be able to escape this event even if they have all the greatest resources, the end is certain and inevitable.

Losing a father or mother is normal and is within the natural order of human life, what is not correct is the opposite, when parents lose their children. And the pain becomes threefold when this happens, because in this way nature is not fulfilling its role correctly. Unfortunately, in our day, due to the waves of violence that have taken over our cities, we see this happening in many families that live surrounded by drugs, prostitution, trafficking and all kinds of marginalization that terribly corrupt our young people in a society without security and protection from the authorities.

The world is modernizing with each passing minute, however it cannot keep up with the extraordinary speed of time and is always positioned a few steps behind what it holds in the future. And what we call the future is just new projects that time will create for each one of us.

1 - Time to be Born and Time to Die

On the day my late father died I was only thirteen years old. I was at home that night, preparing to go to a party with some friends, when the terrible news was given to my family by phone, as he was in another city undergoing treatment to cure a serious heart problem. We all started to cry and were desperate because we didn't have the resources to go to the place where his body was being veiled.

I was quiet for a few hours in the small, narrow courtyard of the humble house where I lived with my mother and brothers, my friends gave me their condolences and recommended that I stay with the family at that difficult time, but I reflected on what Solomon said about the time of be born, grow and die. I remembered that as a son I fully fulfill my role as a son with him, because I was always the most attached, the most attentive, caring and present in his life, I hardly stayed away from him and concluded that we were even with each other.

I got up from where I was and told colleagues that nothing would change in my plans to go to that party that night. To the admiration of some and scandal to others, I went dancing, drinking and smoking with my group until dawn. Do you know what makes people cry desperately when they lose their parents or a relative to death? It is the burden of conscience.

Most do not give them the love, attention, affection, respect, dedication that they deserve and only after they leave for the afterlife do they blame them for everything they did not do before. If we give our family, friends and loved ones all our affection in life when they leave, we will not feel remorse.

I usually call people who cry during a wake of hypocrites, because their tears represent the weight of conscience for what they cowardly relaxed in doing or providing to the deceased who remains there, inert, lying already without the breath of life in that coffin.

Therefore, it is the duty of every parent, child, relative, friend, to demonstrate to those who claim to love as much attention as possible now, while still breathing and not during the last goodbye.

2 - Time to Plant and Time to Harvest

Most people do not take into account their actions and do not consider that every seed planted bears good or bad fruits that will one day need to be harvested. There is a biblical proverb that says, "He who plants hawthorn will reap briers," and that is a great truth. It is no use to go around spreading evil and mistakenly think that the result of this is to reap the kindness of people, we need to be aware of reality.

When writing this proverb, Solomon certainly had in mind this type of person who hurts others with his attitudes and then forgets or pretends to forget, hoping to receive something good from them or from others like him.

But Christ himself said that we should give to others exactly what we would like to receive. If we give contempt, we will be despised, if we betray those who have placed trust in us, we will also be betrayed, if we steal we will be stolen, if we hurt, someone will someday also hurt us.

But if we give love, sincerity, trust, sincerity, justice ... We will reap equally in the same way and in the same amount. Therefore, we must think carefully about what we do against our neighbors, because the harvest will be right, good or bad.

3 - Time to kill and time to heal

Perhaps someone will ask, "Time to kill?" Yes, just that. The term "killing" here does not refer to a crime, a literal murder, but one in which we are capable of causing emotional death. Or someone else's sentimental. For example, I have loved and been loved, I have fallen in love and been the target of many women's passion during my youth.

And I have left a crowd of disappointed women behind me. I speak this truthfully and not to exalt myself. On other occasions it was I who suffered from unrequited love and felt in my chest the pain of a rejected passion. This is also a way of killing someone, taking their pleasure from life and throwing them into the darkness of sadness and loneliness, because the disappointment of love is not easy to endure and there are those who can never overcome it.

But of course, the term used by the writer of Ecclesiastes can, yes, be applied to "kill" someone literally, that is, when one person leads another to death due to something he has caused him. A typical example of this is the suicide caused by several people in the name of a rejected love.

The truth is that the term "time to kill" must lead us to understand that there will be a right time for every thing or situation to occur during our existences in this world where we are not sure what will happen to us in a few milliseconds.

The same thing can be considered in relation to "time to heal", because if at a certain moment we feel ready to hurt or disappoint someone, after a while we can repent and try to correct our mistake with a sincere request for forgiveness.

4 - Time to Knock Down and Time to Build

What can we understand by "Overthrowing and Building" in the expression used by wise King Solomon when writing chapter three of his book Ecclesiastes? Was he referring to a building or a tree? You can put these examples in question, but the main target of your words is directly linked to "throw to the ground"

Or "Lift" a multitude of other things. When we harm someone in some way, we are causing them to fall, whether personal, financial, social, spiritual or moral. According to your wise perspective there will always be a time when we will be responsible for building or destroying something or someone.

Let us stop for a moment and think about everything we have done in the past and see if we were in any way responsible for the destruction of someone. Do we then extend our hands to this person and try to put them on their feet? As the sage said, there is time for everything, one day to do good and another to do evil.

5 - Time to cry and time to laugh, time to mourn and dance

How is the dear reader at this very moment, crying with sadness or laughing with happiness? Certainly your time in life is not the same as mine, or that of others. However, each of us will experience similar situations, because as the saying goes, "one day it is hunting and the other is hunting."

Whoever is sad at this moment, tomorrow may be jumping for joy. Those who smile will cry and regret something bad that happened to them. Time is in charge of always providing us with the other side of the coin the next day, so let us always be alert to this truth.

6 - Time to Spread Stones and Time to Gather them

The term used by the preacher in Ecclesiastes is related to the gathering of people and not exactly "stones". Sometimes, we feel the need to unite with someone, to live a great love, a passion or friendship. Other times, we get tired of the relationship and wish to have our freedom back, preferring solitude. Another definition for the term used by the sage is that there is a certain time.

Sometimes we find ourselves surrounded by several people, in other situations we find ourselves alone and alone. These ups and downs in our lives are the Creator's way of not letting us fall into the existential routine, always experiencing the same things and enjoying the same existential fall.

For love, he decided that the life of each of his creatures would be made up of moments, instants, fractions of small news that would allow them to never have the same day, nor the same night all the time.

7 - Time to Embrace and Time to Get Away

I don't know if the reader is like me, maybe it is quite different, but I am a type of person who changes his attitude from one minute to another. Perhaps because of Cancer, as Astrology says that those born under this sign are temperamental, impulsive, volatile and easily change their mood.

Well, I'm not sure to what extent this is true, but of one thing I am completely sure: "My emotions were very successful. There are times when I fervently wish to be able to count on the company of children, friends and relatives.

But there are times when staying at home alone within four walls is the best option for me. Solomon understood these things. A man who owned three hundred wives and seven hundred lovers knew for sure how stressful it was to have to put up with them all the time, because there is a bag to support such a routine. Imagine going to bed with the same women, practicing the same sex, hearing the same subjects, feeling the same pleasure all the time? Mercy! There is also the case of certain friends who suddenly break their friendship with us and we are perplexed, without understanding anything.

What happens is that at that moment time is taking charge of changing things and we need to be aware of that. Holding a grudge against people because of the changes that occur in their lives is not an intelligent attitude, after all, they are not guilty of anything.

The only person responsible for our interior or exterior changes is time, he is the one who plays with our feelings, moods and everything we are depends on his will. Time decides, chooses, selects and executes everything it wants, because God so determined it to do.

8 - *Time to Search and Time to Quit Searching*

Have you ever missed something important in life that you wanted to find again and then got tired, let it go and forgot? What led you to give up on insisting on finding something that suddenly disappeared from your sight was time, it changed the rules of the game and freed you from that feeling of loss, it showed you a new horizon, new perspectives, made you move on front.

Dear reader, understand that nothing will remain tomorrow exactly as it was today, just as what we are experiencing today was not like yesterday. Right now you can be loving and being loved.

But in twenty-four hours your feeling or that person who is the symbol of your happiness may have changed, to a state above or below what you are now. Nothing remains forever. Even life itself is not eternal, it ends, it has an expiration date. Some people don't understand this.

And when confronted with a separation, when they lose someone with whom they have shared their lives for decades, they go into shock and the collapse of that unexpected loss leads them to suicide.

Living a relationship without first realizing that nothing in this world remains forever is a mistake, as this is the natural course of things in this world, everything comes to an end at a certain time.

As I mentioned earlier, on the day of my brother's funeral I was observing the suffering of his wife and daughters in the last goodbye. They never prepared for that moment when they would part with him. Now, we are not stones, nor eternal in the human form that we exist on this planet, one day our bodies will grow old and stop functioning.

So, why despair? As I said before, it is natural for children to lose their parents. There will always be a time to look for something or someone that has marked our lives in an extraordinary way and a time to give up on finding or having her by our side, because the time will come for separation.

9 - Time to Save and Time to Throw Away

How many things have we missed in life? How many wonderful people did it take for us to part with them during the course of our lives? How much do we keep or throw away, whether material goods or not? For that is what the wise Solomon wanted to explain.

There is time to keep something or someone in our lives and time to dispose of them. We must never cling to what we have as if we will never part with it, because everything in this life is fleeting. People, goods, relationships, everything passes and one day it will cease to exist. So, let's be realistic about that.

10 - Time to Tear and Time to Sew — We can replace the term "Rip" with "Undo" and "Sew" with "Redo or Concert".

There are times in our lives that we build various types of interpersonal relationships that range from simple friendship to dating, engagement, marriage, diverse, professional societies and endless other ways. However, the moment of separation will always come and we need to be ready for when that happens, as there is time for the beginning of these relationships and time for their end.

I clearly remember the day that my older brother created a partnership with a friend and opened a tractor sales and recovery company here in my city. The prospects were good and productive, however, after five years the two fell out and ended the partnership.

Pain and sadness at seeing his dream go down the drain led to a deep depression to the point that he suffered two strokes in the same year. While he was languishing, the former partner grew financially and further increased the revolt that burned in his chest.

This resulted in a deep depression that led him to have a serious illness in his heart and eventually led to his death. Holding on to what we have in this world, whether material goods or not, is a big mistake, because time will force us to have to give up all these things, when we least expect it.Suddenly, the moment will come to do or dispose of something that we build, create, conquer. So, if from now on we understand this, let us always be prepared for such changes, because time will take care of bringing us such surprises.

11 - Time to Talk and Time to Shut Up

There are people who seem to have no control over their own language and being around them is not easy.

In addition to what they usually comment on the lives of others, they spread false rumors, do not know how to keep secrets and are frowned upon by everyone. On the uncontrolled language, the apostle James stated:

"Now, we put a brake on the horses' mouths, so that they will obey us; and we manage to direct your whole body.

See also the ships that, being so big, and carried with impetuous winds, turn themselves with a very small rudder wherever the will of the one who governs them wants.

So the tongue is also a small member, and it boasts great things. See how big a forest a small fire burns.

The tongue is also a fire; as a world of iniquity, the tongue is placed among our members, and contaminates the whole body, and ignites the course of nature, and is ignited by hell.

Because the whole of nature, both of wild beasts and birds, both of reptiles and sea animals, tame and was tamed by human nature;

But no man can tame the tongue. It is an evil that cannot be stopped; it is full of deadly venom.

With it we bless God and Father, and with it we curse men, made in the likeness of God. From the same mouth come blessing and cursing. My brethren, these things ought not so to be." James 3: 3-10

According to his words, the human language must be restrained by its owner or simply be compared to a fire in a forest that will burn everything in front of it, a bleak and uncontrolled fire, causing destruction wherever it goes.

In fact, people whose language control does not exist separate great friendships, deeply hurt others, create strife and irreparable diverse situations. Such individuals are popularly known as gossip, loose tongues, soft mouths, ... Such titles try to give them an adequate reference to their shameful attitudes towards the society where they live, considering them as people who cannot be trusted secrets. In reality there is immense confusion in this regard because some believe that talking too much demonstrates communicability, however, about this we read in Scripture, that:

"He who keeps his mouth keeps his soul, but he who opens his lips a lot is destroyed." **Proverbs 13: 3**

Whoever talks too much ends up revealing what should remain hidden and incriminating others who trusted him. The constant opening of the lips is not even a sign of intelligence, it does not show wisdom, nor does it characterize someone as communicative.

According to a recent survey by a group of North American psychologists, people with a higher IQ tend to choose to live in isolation, loneliness and little speaking are its main characteristics. It is interesting that since the most remote times of civilizations this was already known to men like Solomon and others who studied human behavior.

People with extreme wisdom know when to speak and be silent, barely open their mouths, give more importance to listening and learning than teaching or commenting on certain subjects. Unlike the wise, fools talk a lot, comment a lot, express their views too much and want to be heard at any cost. They are extremely boring, tiring and enduring them is a real martyrdom.

During my youth one of my main rules for dating a young girl or maintaining friendships was to demand that they not talk too much. I never got along with people whose language was out of control, because I was uncomfortable with the exaggeration of words in my ear. I have always given greater importance to the more timid, less talkative, less expressive, because this is the strong mark of intellectuals.

The biggest names found in science, technology, and in the other areas of studies responsible for the expansion of modern knowledge come from people whose personality has a reserved and largely lonely behavior. Few are those who demonstrate to be expressive in their words, most of them do not even like to give interviews because they are averse to questions and to answer them.

12 - Time to Hate and Time to Love

As a young man, I left a huge number of broken-hearted girls behind, as I was always very flirtatious and fickle in my generally short-lived relationships. One of my main marks, which little by little became known to the girls and that made them turn away from me for repudiating such a character, was the sudden discontent in the relationship.

After a short period of dating I was already dissatisfied and left for another one, in most cases leaving behind a girl with tears in her eyes and that immensely tarnished my reputation due to the inconsequential posture and for not showing the slightest feeling towards them at that moment of pain and suffering. This was not just my posture, as several other people acted and still do the same today.

There are those who initiate a relationship and remain in it for decades, some even die alongside their first love. But, people like me cannot live forever side by side with the same passion, the same friendships, in the same routine. There are those who can't even stay in the same job for a long time and similar to nomads constantly change places, filling the pages of their professional cards with the CNPJ of this or that Company.

There is the right time to love someone, things, objects, places, the profession, the place where we operate, interpersonal relationships ... And there is the time to feel tired of it all. Because of that friendships come to an end, marriages and friendships end, people stop hanging out together and even family members go years without seeing each other. The term "Love" and "Hate" used by Solomon can be changed to "Desire and Reject".

13 - Time to Fight and Time to Peace

Both in relation to the political and social world as well as in the family aspect, in interpersonal, professional relationships and in general there is the right time for struggles and peace. Social disputes are caused by competition between different groups that want to occupy a better and more expressive position. Those at the bottom of the pyramid want to climb to the top.

Even when we participate in a public exam, an entrance exam, we run for a new job vacancy, a family inheritance, a position of authority within our homes and many other factors similar to this one we are in a constant battle. However, there will always be a time when we will put an end to these situations and peace will reign. We, human beings, bring by nature the light and darkness lodged within our being.

And these two ends of our human character lead us to live in constant dispute internally and externally, humanly and spiritually, against each other and dissatisfied with what we are or have, always wanting a little more than we have, to go beyond our limits. But if on the one hand it seems to be a flaw in our personality, it ends up resulting in growth as people with free will to evolve in all areas of our existence.

If today we can fly like birds, run like ostriches, communicate with those on the other side of the world, climb the outer space and get to know the vast Universe and its planets, it is because we did not stand still watching time pass in vain, but we went capable of dissatisfaction with our old way of life we decided to get up and go to the fight, to fight for the modernity that we currently conquer.

If countries go to war and kill each other because of their commercial and political ambitions, it is because each of them seeks their own economic growth, however, we see that from time to time they quiet down, give themselves time to rest and only then return to fight. There the words of the sage are fulfilled when he affirms that there is a time for everything under heaven, even a time of struggle and a time of peace.

Second Part

Concepts About True Love

Regarding true love, the apostle Paul wrote:

"Even if I spoke the languages of men and angels, and had no love, it would be like the ringing metal or the ringing bell. And even if he had the gift of prophecy, and knew all the mysteries and all the science, and even though he had all the faith, in such a way that he carried the mountains, and had no love, nothing would be.

And even if I distributed all my fortune to support the poor, and even if I gave up my body to be burned, and had no love, none of that would benefit me. Love is suffering, it is benign; love is not envious; love does not treat lightly, it does not puff up.

He does not behave indecently, does not pursue his interests, is not irritated, does not suspect evil. Do not take leave with injustice, but take leave with truth. Everything suffers, everything believes, everything hopes, everything endures."

1 Corinthians 13: 1-7

The so-called modern world started to confuse true love with the passing passions that suddenly appear in the hearts of this volatile generation and in a short time it dissolves like a mere fog even comparing it with the sexual act.

I t is common to hear the phrase "let's make love", as if one thing is compared to another. Will a prostitute who goes to bed with a client who is paying for her body also be making "love" during sex? Should a woman during rape, the child be raped, the intimate relationship between two irresponsible teenagers, should such acts be seen equally as a form of love?

The term "love" has never been more trivialized by humanity than in this century. People fall in love and through this volatile and irresponsible feeling they practice all kinds of madness and still dare to claim that they are in love. However, here are the main characteristics of true love:

1 - Even if I speak the language of men and angels ...

We could substitute the apostle's first sentence for "Even if I had the glory of an angel ... "Paul explains that even if he possessed the radiance of a celestial being if he did not bring true love within him, it would be useless. This means that a person's outward appearance does not prove or reveal his true character.

We have all met people who were apparently loyal, trustworthy and because of their false appearance they deceived us and ended up becoming the reason for our biggest disappointment.

It doesn't matter how we present ourselves to the world, but what we really are internally, our moral character, our commitment to the truth and the constant desire for justice.

Taking into account this expression of the apostle, we can refer to what God said to Samuel, when he was enchanted with the physical beauty of Eliab, son of Jesse, when he was sent to choose and anoint the new king of Israel to replace Saul:

"And it came to pass, when they entered, that he saw Eliab, and said, Surely the anointed one is before the Lord. But the Lord said to Samuel, Pay no attention to his appearance, nor to the greatness of his stature, because I have rejected him; because the Lord does not see how he sees man, for man sees what is before the eyes, but the Lord looks at the heart. " 1 Samuel 16: 6,7

It is common for human beings to pay more attention to the external appearance of other people and to leave it at the bottom of mind to consider their moral character expressed by their attitudes, through their words, ideas, points of view and their behavior as a whole. Samuel made the first mistake in choosing Saul to reign over Israel just because of his physical appearance, because in the old judge and prophet's conception a king should have beauty as the main characteristic.

After being disappointed with Saul when he realizes that he is unable to obey divine ordinances Samuel is sent to the house of Jesse to anoint one of his sons as the new king who should rule his people in Saul's place and once again wanted to make the choice through his prejudiced analysis, taking into account only the candidate's physical appearance and not his moral side and the willingness to hear and obey the voice of God.

It was then that the Lord clarified to him that he did not look only at the outer side of human beings, was not deceived by appearance, but probed the heart of each person in particular and considered their true purposes. When he saw that God chose David as a substitute for Saul, a thin, red-haired young man. looking completely opposite to what he imagined so he would sit on the throne and reign over the Israelites.

He was very disappointed. He certainly must have wondered what the Lord had seen in him. This occurs a lot within our churches, when a worker who in the eyes of many is too inexperienced to occupy a certain ministerial position and is suddenly called to the function, when there are others more qualified for the function, causing enormous discontent.

As much as it hurts to witness these things happen in our midst, it is important to remember what was said by God to Samuel, "Pay no attention to his appearance or the greatness of his stature, because I have rejected him; because the Lord does not see how he sees man, for man sees what is before the eyes, but the Lord looks at the heart. "

Through the mouth of the prophet Isaiah, he warned:

"For just as the heavens are higher than the earth, so are my ways higher than your ways, and my thoughts higher than your thoughts." Isaiah 55: 9

Valuing people for their appearance is a form of judgment in relation to others endowed with less physical beauty, it is imagining that an individual only has good qualities if they are beautiful, it is calculating the size of someone's intelligence by their beauty. In this regard, Jesus warned:

"Do not judge, lest you be judged. Because with the judgment with which you judge you will be judged, and with the measure with which you have measured they will measure you." Matthew 7: 1,2

How many immensely intelligent people lost a job in a certain company, during a selection, because they lacked physical beauty or because of their skin color? Many entrepreneurs no longer have real geniuses on their staff just because recruiting agencies give priority to the candidates' appearance.

And not their ability.

2 - Even if I had the gift of prophecy ...

During the years that I worked as a pastor in several evangelical communities I could see the enormous dispute between brothers in the faith in wanting to have greater spiritual prominence in the middle of the church, among them those endowed with the gifts of speaking in strange languages and prophecies.

Those to whom the Holy Spirit gave the gift of speaking in tongues stood up in the middle of the church, during services, and began to speak in a strange and incomprehensible language, causing much confusion for those who had not yet converted to the Gospel and, therefore, they did not know such a thing.

At other times it was the prophets who made revelations to this or that brother, claiming that it was God who commanded them to give such a warning. In that I saw many couples split up in the name of the divine warning that that union was not the Lord's will, in addition to other things. As for these things, also seen by Paul in the troubled church in Corinth, we read:

"He who speaks in an unknown language builds himself up, but he who prophesies builds up the church.

And I want you all to speak in tongues, but much more than you prophesy; because he who prophesies is greater than he who speaks in tongues, unless he also interprets so that the church may receive edification.

And now, brethren, if I come to you speaking in tongues, what would I do to you, if I did not speak to you or through revelation, or science, or prophecy, or doctrine?

Likewise, if inanimate things that make sound, whether flute or zither, do not form distinct sounds, how will one know what is played with the flute or the zither?

Because if the trumpet sounds uncertain, who will prepare for battle? So you too, if you do not speak very intelligible words with your tongue, how will you understand what is said? because you will be as if speaking to the air.

There are, for example, so many kinds of voices in the world, and none of them are meaningless. But if I ignore the meaning of the voice, I will be barbaric to the one I speak to, and the speaker will be barbaric to me.

So also, as you desire spiritual gifts, seek to abound in them, for the edification of the church. Therefore, whoever speaks in an unknown language, pray that he can interpret it.

Because if I pray in an unknown language, my spirit prays well, but my understanding is fruitless.

What will I do then? I will pray with the spirit, but I will also pray with the understanding; I will sing with the spirit, but I will also sing with the understanding. Otherwise, if you bless with the spirit, how will you say what takes the place of indouto, Amen, about your thanksgiving, since you do not know what you say?

Because you really give thanks well, but the other is not built. I give thanks to my God, because I speak more languages than you all. However, first I want to speak five words in the church in my own intelligence, so that I can also instruct others.

Than ten thousand words in an unknown language. Brothers, do not be children in understanding, but children in malice, and adults in understanding. *It is written in the law: By people of other languages, and by other lips, I will speak to these people.*

And yet they will not hear me, says the Lord. So that tongues are a sign, not for the faithful, but for the unbelievers; and prophecy is not a sign for the unbelievers, but for the faithful.

If, then, the whole church congregates in one place, and everyone speaks in tongues, and the uneducated or unfaithful come in, will they not say that you are mad?

But if everyone prophesies, and someone who is unfaithful or unfaithful enters, everyone is convinced, everyone is judged.

And therefore, the secrets of your heart are made manifest, and thus, casting itself upon your face, you will worship God, publishing that God is truly among you.

What will you do then, brothers? When you come together, each of you has a psalm, has a doctrine, has a revelation, has a tongue, has an interpretation. Everything is done for edification.

And if anyone speaks in an unknown language, do it for two, or at most three, and in turn, and have an interpreter.

But if there is no interpreter, be quiet in the church, and talk to yourself, and to God. And speak two or three prophets, and the others judge. But, if the other, who is seated, something is revealed, shut up the first.

For you will all be able to prophesy, one after the other; so that everyone learns, and everyone is comforted. And the spirits of the prophets are subject to the prophets. Because God is not a God of confusion, but of peace, as in all the churches of the saints. 1 Corinthians 14: 4-33

The use of the gifts given by the Spirit within the churches is real, true and necessary for their edification, but it must be done with decency and order, which was not happening in Corinth.

There, there was a real dispute between those who spoke in tongues and those who prophesied, disputing to know which of the two sides had the most important gift. Then the apostle clarifies that whoever prophesies edifies the church, but whoever speaks in foreign languages without proper interpretation only cause confusion.

3 - Know all the mysteries and all the science ...

Generally those who work in medicine and science are incredulous about the existence of God and tend to criticize those who believe so, attributing to themselves the merit of their deeds. However, all the human wisdom that led us to so many conquests comes from the Lord.

It was he who endowed us with all the intelligence and in different ways perfected us so that we could reach the highest point of all the scientific and technological knowledge that we have today in the face from the earth. Regarding true wisdom, Solomon wrote:

"... Because the Lord gives wisdom; from your mouth comes knowledge and understanding. He reserves true wisdom for the upright. Shield is for those who walk in sincerity.

To keep the paths of judgment. He will preserve the way of his saints. Then you will understand justice, judgment, equity and all good paths. For when wisdom enters your heart, and knowledge is pleasing to your soul. Good wisdom will keep you and intelligence will keep you. " **Proverbs 2: 6-11**

As much as man in the fullness of his deeds can fill his heart with pride and affirm in a good tone that God does not exist, he will never be able to prove this affirmation, because nature itself and the Universe above his head give evidence that only a Being endowed with infinite strength and power could create all the things that end up becoming objects of admiration in your mortal eyes.

According to what we read above, true wisdom consists simply in believing that the Lord exists, in worshiping him, obeying and following his advice. That is, in fact, having wisdom. Human pride causes spiritual blindness in skeptics who cannot see a foot in front of their nose and try to explain the origin of the heavens, the earth and life with their absurd and unsubstantiated theories. The Scriptures tell us that everything was created through the Word of an Almighty God, and just look around or up and we will see the truth of this statement.

4 - Even if I had all the faith ...

It is true that some people have a greater faith than others and because of that they receive more answers from God and are more blessed. However, Paul explains that even if he had a living and effective faith if he did not have a truly pure, sincere love in his heart, and the way God requires every Christian would be of no use. The love cited by the apostle in this biblical text has nothing to do with the feeling of passion or sexual desire that the modern world paints.

Blue and preaches on the posters of life, shows in soap operas, practices within four walls or teaches the new generation the false idea to love. What is being discussed here is the purest love that comes from on high, from the Lord to our hearts. And only if it exists in each person's heart is it worth having faith.

Someone may have the power to remove the "mountains" from his life by praying with an unshakable faith, but without the presence of true love he can become selfish, presumptuous and petty, using this gift only for his own benefit and not of others, as God requires us to do. Our Heavenly Father's will is for us to act as he did, giving the life of his only Son to allow us to be free from the chains of sin.

Thinking about the good of others is the most complete and perfect way to love and it was God himself who taught us this when he sent Jesus to Calvary. Only by giving ourselves to our fellow men can we imitate the Most High in the fullness of his infinite mercy.

In no other way will we be able to copy their acts on behalf of humanity, only through an unreserved, pure and sincere donation. This is the meaning of the word "love", it means to surrender, to give, to serve others.

And it is she who gives meaning to everything we practice in this world, especially when we practice faith and any other gift that has been given to us by the Holy Spirit.

5 - And even if I distributed all my fortune to the poor ...

This statement by Paul makes us think of thousands of people who have never decided on Christ, but practice works of charity towards the poor, mistakenly thinking that such contributions guarantee the salvation eternal.

Many celebrities send millionaire checks every month to help orphanages, NGOs, charities, support scientific discoveries to cure new diseases, etc ... And firmly believe that they will be pleasing the heart of God for their generosity. However, Paul explains that even when doing all these things if you do not bring true love into you, it is in vain.

We know that the vast majority of millionaires who practice such acts of generosity do not do it for nothing, but there is always behind all this an ambitious claim to promote themselves. A great example of this we could see during this Covid-19 pandemic, when several entrepreneurs and private sector institutions, banks, donated millions to help fight the virus, however, they insisted on showing their achievements to society through the media. in order to promote itself.

When we practice charity and play the trombone to show everyone what we have just done, we prove that we did not do it out of love for our fellowmen, but to receive applause or reward. On the right way to practice charity, Christ taught us:

"Be careful not to do your' works of justice 'before others to be seen by them. If you do, you will have no reward from Heavenly Father.

"Therefore, when you give alms, do not announce it with trumpets, as hypocrites do in synagogues and on the streets, in order to be honored by others. I assure you that they have already received their full reward.

But when you give alms, let your left hand not know what the right hand is doing, so that you can help in secret. And your Father, who sees what is done in secret, will reward you ".

"And when you pray, don't be like the hypocrites. They like to stand in prayer in synagogues and on corners, in order to be seen by others. I assure you that they have already received their full reward."

Matthew 6: 1-5

The Lord does not like us to be hypocrites like the Pharisees of his day, as they insisted on showing everyone in the streets that they were practicing some charity in order to be considered as sympathetic and merciful. Such attitudes irritated the Son of God who defied them by calling them false and self-*serving, as we read in the biblical text below:*

"Woe to you, teachers of the law and Pharisees, hypocrites! You close the kingdom of heaven before men! You yourselves do not enter, nor do you let in those who would like to do so.

"Woe to you, teachers of the law and Pharisees, hypocrites! You devour widows' houses and, in disguise, say long prayers. That is why you will be punished more severely.

"Woe to you, teachers of the law and Pharisees, hypocrites, because you travel across land and sea to make a convert, and when you do, you make him twice as much a son of hell as you.

"Woe to you, blind guides! For you say, 'If anyone swears by the sanctuary, it means nothing; but if someone swears by the gold of the sanctuary, he is bound by his oath'.

Blind fools! Which is more important: gold or the sanctuary that sanctifies gold?

You also say: 'If someone swears by the altar, it means nothing; but if anyone swears by the offer that is on him, he is bound by his oath '. Blind! Which is more important: the offering, or the altar that sanctifies the offering? Therefore, he who swears by the altar, swears by him and by everything that is on him.

And he who swears by the sanctuary, swears by him and by the one who lives there.

And he who swears by heaven, swears by the throne of God and by him who sits on it.

"Woe to you, teachers of the law and Pharisees, hypocrites! You tithe mint, dill and cumin, but you have neglected the most important precepts of the law: justice, mercy and faithfulness. You must practice these things, without omitting those.

Blind guides! You strain a mosquito and swallow a camel.

"Woe to you, teachers of the law and Pharisees, hypocrites! You clean the outside of the cup and plate, but inside they are full of greed and greed.

Blind Pharisee! Clean the inside of the cup and plate first, so that the outside is also clean.

"Woe to you, teachers of the law and Pharisees, hypocrites! You are like whitewashed graves: beautiful on the outside, but inside you are full of bones and all kinds of filth.

So are you: on the outside you seem righteous to the people, but on the inside you are full of hypocrisy and evil.

"Woe to you, teachers of the law and Pharisees, hypocrites! You build the tombs of the prophets and adorn the monuments of the just.

And they say: "If we had lived in the time of our ancestors, we would not have taken part with them in the shedding of the blood of the prophets".

Thus, you testify against yourselves that you are the descendants of those who murdered the prophets.

So finish filling up the measure of your ancestors' sin!

"Snakes! Race of vipers! How will you escape condemnation to hell?

Therefore, I am sending you prophets, sages and teachers. You will kill and crucify some; others will flog in your synagogues and chase you from city to city.

And so all the righteous blood shed on the earth will fall on you, from the blood of Just Abel, to the blood of Zacharias, son of Baraquias, whom you murdered between the sanctuary and the altar.

I assure you that all of this will come to this generation." Matthew 23: 13-36

Religious hypocrisy, as well as any other form of falsehood, is combated, rejected and considered an abomination before the holy gaze of God who hates deception. For this same reason, the apostle Paul emphasized that even if he donated all his goods to the poor, without true love in his heart, it would be of no avail.

6 - Love is a Sufferer....

Aqui não se trata do sofrer pela paixão sentida por alguém.

But a collective suffering, focused on the needs of others, the pain that the world feels overtaken by financial and spiritual misery, seeing thousands of people lost without God and without salvation, walking blindly into the abyss. Those who have the true love of God within themselves cannot be at peace when they see their fellows lying in the gutter, hungry, naked and barefoot, sick with body and soul, without any hope.

I tend to say in my lectures that being religious is no guarantee that someone has the characteristics of God in their lives, as there are many unbelievers who provide more help to those in need than certain Christians and do it with true compassion, a pity that without conversion in Christ their actions end up being empty and in vain. The parable below quoted by Jesus gives us a practical example of this:

"A man was coming down from Jerusalem to Jericho, when he fell into the hands of robbers. These took off his clothes, beat him and left him almost dead.

A priest happened to be coming down the same road. When he saw the man, he passed the other side.

And so too is a Levite; when she got to the place and saw him, she passed the other side. But a Samaritan, traveling, came to where the man was, and when he saw him, he had pity on him.

He approached, bandaged his wounds, pouring wine and oil on them. Then he put him on his own animal, took him to an inn and took care of him. The next day, he gave the host two denarii and said: 'Take care of him. When I get back I'll pay you all the expenses you have.

"Which of these three do you think was next to the man who fell into the hands of the robbers?

"The one who had mercy on him," replied the law expert. Jesus said to him, "Go and do the same." Luke 10: 30-37

7 - Love is benign ...

Being benign also means having the following qualities:

Kindness, Benevolence, Mercy, ability to forgive, never hold grudges, not be vindictive, be sincere, patient, feel compassion, affectionate, charitable, pious, dignified ...

True love gives its possessor all these qualities and makes him extremely humble, loving and able to express the loving qualities of his Creator.

8 - Love is not envious ...

Envy is not part of the divine qualities, but it represents the fallen personality of Satan. It was this flaw in Lucifer's character that led him to want to cast the Most High from his throne and take his place in heaven. Due to this unfortunate presumption, he was banished forever from paradise and transformed into an aberration along with those who chose to follow his example.

"You were in Eden, the garden of God; your covering was of all precious stones: Sardonia, topaz, diamond, turquoise, onyx, jasper, sapphire, carbuncle, emerald and gold; your drums and your fife were made in you; the day you were created they were prepared. You were the cherubim, anointed to cover.

And I established you; on the holy mountain of God you were walking among the flushed stones. You were perfect in your ways, from the day you were created, until iniquity was found in you. In the multiplication of your trade they filled your interior with violence, and you sinned.

That is why I threw you, profaned, from the mountain of God, and made you perish, O covering cherub, from among the flushed stones.

Your heart was lifted up because of your beauty, you corrupted your wisdom because of your radiance; I threw you down to the earth, before the kings I set you, so that they may look at you.

By the multitude of your iniquities, by the injustice of your trade, you have profaned your sanctuaries; I therefore caused a fire to come out of you, which consumed you and turned you into ashes on the earth, in the eyes of all who see you.

All who know you among the peoples are astonished at you; in great amazement you have become, and will never survive." **Ezekiel 28: 13-19**

Just as Lucifer was strictly punished for standing up against God out of impetuous envy, all human beings who allow themselves to be dominated by this feeling will also destroy themselves.

No envious person will make progress in his life because he who wastes time admiring the evolution of others will never prosper.

9 - Love is neither light nor proud ...

A frivolous person has the following definitions:

"Who behaves foolishly without reflection; foolish. Who judges in advance or without reflecting on what he says. That does not express seriousness or wisdom; irresponsible. Which demonstrates or indicates lightness, lack of seriousness or folly. Inconstant, devoid of constancy; without consistency; fickle."

However, those who allow themselves to be dominated and guided by the true love of God are the opposite of all this and endowed with extreme moral character. Pride is that someone has the following characteristics, completely negative.

"Who owns or denotes pride and arrogance; proud. In which there is grandeur; magnificent, majestic: superb concert. Excessively valued or precious; precious: superb cars. Higher up than the rest: superb mountains."

A superb person is generally arrogant, thinks he is superior to others in moral, physical qualities, in economic power and never admits to feeling equal or less than anyone. However, those who have true love in them never look at their peers vertically, from top to bottom, but horizontally, equaling the other people around them. Christ acted in this way by becoming a man and choosing to be born into a humble and wealthy family.

Since God abdicated his throne where he was worshiped and served by thousands of heavenly angels, he came down and lived among the poorest and most rejected by the society of his time. In the end he gave his human life on a cross for everyone. At any time or place, rich and poor, whites, blacks or any other ethnicity can accept him and, by letting this life go to live with him in paradise.

This must be the characteristic of the true Christian, acting as his Master, never feeling superior to others, but loving everyone without distinction as Jesus did. Paul categorically states that love is neither envious nor proud, making it clear that this must be the main characteristic of those who love.

10 - Don't behave indecently ...

Once a young woman from the evangelical congregation where I served as a minister of the Gospel came to me to ask if it was right for her boyfriend to touch her breasts and intimate parts during the moments when they kissed. I immediately made it very clear to that girl of only sixteen that this attitude was dishonorable and that it was not part of the courtship.

Of course, we live in a world where everything is allowed among young people, from bold caresses to free sex, but none of this is mandatory, accept whoever you want. But Christian customs must be different from those practiced abroad, in a lost society and without fear of God.

Our children must be educated from an early age to behave like a people bought and washed in the blood of Christ and not to copy the terrible example of the infidels. Let us remember the recommendations made by the Lord our God to Moses, when he was preparing to introduce the Israelites to the promised land:

"The LORD spoke to Moses, saying, Speak to the children of Israel, and say to them, I am the Lord your God: You will not do according to the works of the land of Egypt, in which you dwelt. Nor will you do according to the works of the land of Canaan, to which I take you, nor will you walk in its statutes.

You will do according to my judgments, and you will keep my statutes, to walk in them. I am the Lord your God. Therefore, you will keep my statutes and my judgments; who, watching a man, will live for them. I am the Lord.

No man will approach any relative of his flesh to discover his nakedness. I am the Lord.

You will not discover the nakedness of your father and your mother: she is your mother; you will not discover its nakedness.

You will not discover the nakedness of your father's wife; it's your father's nudity.

The nudity of your sister, your father's daughter, or your mother's daughter, born at home or outside, your nudity you will not discover.

You will not discover the nakedness of your son's daughter, or your daughter's daughter; because it's your nakedness.

The nakedness of your father's wife's daughter, generated from your father (she is your sister), your nakedness you will not discover.

You will not discover the nakedness of your father's sister; she is related to your father.

You will not discover the nakedness of your mother's sister; because she is related to your mother. You will not discover the nakedness of your father's brother; you will not approach your wife; she is your aunt. You will not discover the nakedness of your daughter-in-law. She is your son's wife; you will not discover its nakedness. You will not discover the nakedness of your brother's wife; it is your brother's nakedness.

You will not discover the nakedness of a woman and her daughter. You shall not take your son's daughter or your daughter's daughter to discover her nakedness; kin are; evil is.

And you will not take a woman together with your sister, to make her your rival, discovering her nakedness before her in your life.

And you will not reach the woman during the separation from her filth, to discover her nakedness.

Nor will you lie with your neighbor's wife for copulation, to defile yourself with her.

And you shall give none of your descendants to pass through the fire before Molech; and you shall not profane the name of your God. I am the Lord.

You will not lie with a man, as if you were a woman; abomination is.

Nor will you lie down with an animal to defile yourself with it; nor will a woman stand before an animal to gather with it; confusion is.

Do not defile yourself with any of these things; because with all these things the nations that I drive out before you have become defiled. That is why the land is contaminated; and I visit their iniquity, and the land vomits its inhabitants. But you will keep my statutes and my judgments, and none of these abominations will you make, neither the natural nor the foreigner who wanders among you. For all these abominations did the men of this land, who were in it before you; and the land was contaminated. Lest the land vomit you, having defiled it, as the nation that was before you vomited.

However, whoever does any of these abominations, yes, those who do will be cut off from their people. Therefore, you will keep my commandment. Doing none of the abominable practices that were done before you, and do not be defiled by them. I am the Lord your God." Leviticus 18: 1-30

As we can see, the main demand made by God to his people was to stay away from unbelievers and separated from the sinful society of that time so that they would not fall into the same error as they did, for they did not know the Lord and were devil worshipers, idolaters, immorals, adulterers and practiced various other things that led to becoming abominable in the eyes of the Almighty.

In the ordinance of the Most High, it was not for his people to mingle with those people, giving their daughters in marriage to the young Canaanites so that the Israelite blood was not contaminated with their serious sins. In the same way, the Holy Spirit, who inhabits the church, recommends that we do the same. Sheep must be joined to another sheep, as well as a Christian to another Christian.

Dating, marriage and even friendship between the children of the Most High and the world becomes enmity against the Lord. But, for this to be understood in the minds of our children, it is necessary to teach them from an early age, in the first years of life, because in adolescence it becomes impossible for them to assimilate, since they have already been influenced by the media.

Social networks, diverse friendships and teachings contaminated by modern ideology in schools. It is our duty, as parents, to guide our children on how to behave in this world as an authentic Christian.

Without having to follow the bad examples of those who still live imprisoned in their crimes and sins, the enemies of our God and the lost society where we live.

11 - Do not seek your interests ...

A self-serving person never does anything for the sake of others out of love or respect, but behind his actions there is always self-interest. It is completely unfeasible for someone to say that he has given some humanitarian aid if he then expects to receive something in return, because those who are really capable of loving their fellow men do not seek to be rewarded for the good they do, they give themselves spontaneously.

Jesus cited the Pharisees as an example of those who do everything they do publicly in order to have their works recognized by others, wanting to receive applause and to be called kind people. Paul explained that authentic love does not consist in seeking one's own benefit, but in benefiting our fellow men, as this is God's will for his children. Modern society is used to the traditional "give and take", that is, I help you and then you also reach out to me.

However, this is not the attitude of those who claim to know God, because he gave himself on the cross for us all and asked for nothing in return, on the contrary, he brought us the Good News of Salvation, the Gospel of Grace, but he gives us the free agency for us to make the choice to follow it or not. Therefore, let us guide our families from the need to follow the divine demands so that we can keep ourselves free from the punishment of our God, since the moment has already arrived when the cups of his will are already being poured on the inhabitants of the earth, on those who out of sheer rebellion, they defy their excellent power and ridicule their glory and holiness.

The seven angels have already positioned themselves and have been punishing humanity for a long time.

In Revelation, we read:

"And I saw the seven angels, who were before God, and they were given seven trumpets. And another angel came and stood by the altar, having a golden censer; and he was given much incense to put it with the prayers of all the saints on the golden altar, which is before the throne.

And the smoke of the incense rose with the prayers of the saints from the angel's hand to God.

And the angel took the censer, and filled it with fire from the altar, and threw it on the earth; and then there were voices, and thunder, and lightning and earthquakes.

And the seven angels, who had the seven trumpets, prepared to sound them.

And the first angel blew his trumpet, and there was hail and fire mixed with blood, and they were thrown into the land, which was burned in its third part; a third of the trees were burned, and all the green grass was burned.

And the second angel blew the trumpet; and a thing like a great mountain burning with fire was thrown into the sea, and a third of the sea became blood. And a third of the creatures that had life at sea died; and a third of the ships were lost.

And the third angel blew his trumpet, and a great star burning like a torch fell from heaven, and fell on a third of the rivers, and on the springs of the waters.

And the name of the star was Absinthe, and a third of the waters became absinthe, and many men died from the waters, because they became bitter. And the fourth angel blew his trumpet, and a third of the sun, and a third of the moon, and a third of the stars were smitten.

So that a third of them would darken, and a third of the day would not shine, and likewise the night. And I looked, and I heard an angel fly **through the sky, saying with a loud voice: Alas! there! there! of those who dwell on the earth! because of the other voices of the trumpets of the three angels that will still play**. **Revelation 8: 2-13**

12 - Don't get angry, don't suspect badly ...

When we truly and sincerely love our fellow men we know how to be patient with their failures and mistakes, forgiving and always giving them the opportunity to redeem themselves with us. Only those who do not carry this feeling within themselves are unable to act in this way and end up becoming resentful, bitter, vindictive and suspicious people.

The act of suspecting badly demonstrates that an individual does not have the genuine love of God and is driven by selfishness that makes him see only his own existential world, considering himself the only creature on the face of the earth worthy of trust and respect. Such people diminish the importance and value of others, adding to themselves all possible prestige.

13 - Don't play with injustice, but play with truth ...

Genuine love prevents us from acting unjustly with our fellow men, does not admit cowardice, injustice, false testimonies, criticisms or accusations. Whoever acts in this way does not have the love of God within his heart.

Because he does not allow such behavior. This feeling is pure, loyal, faithful, true and never dwells in the midst of falsehood and hypocrisy. Those who have been gifted with this gift are people of high moral value, have a spiritual brilliance so strong that it can be felt by everyone around them.

14 - Everything suffers, everything believes, everything hopes, everything endures.

And finally, true love makes us able to suffer in silence, without murmuring or wanting revenge against those who have hurt us. It leads us to believe that such individuals can change and transform the hatred they feel for us into a sincere and lasting friendship. It teaches us to wait patiently for time to heal the wounds of the soul and comfort our stoned hearts. It makes it possible for us to endure affront without being discouraged and to believe that one day peace will reign where there is discord.

Final Part

Various Concepts

How useless! "says the Master." How useless! Nothing makes sense! "What does man gain from all his work that he struggles under the sun?

Generations come and generations go, but the land remains forever.

The sun rises and the sun sets, and quickly returns to the place from which it rises.

The wind blows south and turns north; goes around and around, always following its course.

All rivers go to the sea, yet the sea never fills; although they always run there, run there again. All things bring tiredness. Man is not able to describe them; the eyes are never satisfied with seeing, nor the ears with hearing.

What was will be, what was done will be done again; there is nothing new under the sun.

Is there anything you can say: "Look! This is new!"? No! It has existed a long time ago; well before our time.

No one remembers those who lived in antiquity, and those who are yet to come will not be remembered by those who come after them. **Ecclesiastes 1: 2-11**

1 - *What do we gain from so much work?*

A good question if we stop to think that we will take nothing on the day of our death. I have already witnessed the wake of many people who lived to accumulate material goods, but at the time of their departure they barely took the body's clothes to the grave and when they left their bodies they went to the other side naked, barefoot and empty-handed. What was the value of so much work, so much fatigue, so much savings and the accumulation of so many riches in this world where they spent only a third of their lives if they went to live eternity with nothing they built here?

They left everything for other people to enjoy, enjoy what they did not struggle to conquer and build. If we look more closely at our lives, we will understand the Thinker's wise words in Ecclesiastes when stating that so much effort to accumulate treasures on earth is wasted time, it is a real idiocy. For this reason, Christ said:

"Do not set up treasures on the land, where moth and rust consume everything, and where thieves mine and steal.

But gather up treasures in the sky, where neither moth nor rust consume, and where thieves neither mine nor steal.

Because where your treasure is, there is also your heart. " **Matthew 6: 19-21**

Where is your heart at this moment, dear reader, in God or in His material wealth? Don't forget that your time in this world is fleeting and you will soon have to leave. Nothing that has accumulated in this short existence can be taken to the grave and still less to the beyond, everything will be left behind.

2 - Generations come and Generations are gone and the land remains ... All rivers go to the sea, but the sea never fills ...

Since the foundation of the world, countless civilizations have existed and continue to exist where several generations lived in them, each one more evolved than the other, but the land remains the same, despite changes in nature.

In this biblical context what the wise man wants to tell us is that the planet is not directly linked to man and his scientific, cultural, political and social evolution, but is independent of these influences, being God the only one who can modify it naturally by the force of your power.

As human beings we can change the land by building cities, through plantations, of different works, but it will remain the same land, the same planet. On the other hand, Solomon tries to explain that we have no power over nature and we can do nothing to change it, although this idea today can be refuted, because due to the action of man and his industries we destroy a lot of it, as for example the ozone layer and several other factors that cause global warming and catastrophic natural incidents.

3 - All things bring tiredness ... The eyes are never satisfied to see, nor the ears to hear ...

This part of the biblical text can be related to the ambition of human beings, their tireless search for wealth, money, material goods ... etc. The constant habit of chasing new conquests makes us dissatisfied with what we have and what we are, always wanting more and more. On the one hand, this can be seen in a positive way.

Because it was because of this natural dissatisfaction of the human race that we evolved and built all the technological and scientific advances that we have today, which would be impossible to achieve if we were a stopped, incredulous and imprisoned generation. in the inertia of just admiring nature and the Universe, helpless, believing that everything was too big or too distant to touch, explore and even in many cases modify them.

Today we fly in spaceships, explore outer space and know what is up there as much as what is down here, on land and within the oceans, we are no longer simple observers, as were those born in past generations, and we we have become universal explorers, no matter how extreme this has brought us.

4 - *What was will be, what was done will be done again; there is nothing new under the sun ...*

This expression by the wise Solomon has caused many theological controversies, mainly among the spiritists who believe he is claiming that reincarnation does exist, which is contested by other religions. Christianity does not claim that there is a possibility that the human soul returns to earth through a new body, however, if we study the Gospels deeply we will see that Christ himself occupied a new physical body when he rose from the dead, in addition to claiming that John was the incarnation of the prophet Elijah. So we read in Matthew 17: 12,13:

"But I tell you, Elijah has already come, and they didn't know him, but they did everything he wanted. So will they also suffer the Son of man. Then the disciples understood that John the Baptist had spoken to them."

In this way, it is understood that in fact there is a possibility that the Spiritist doctrine on reincarnation is true, but the Christian faith insists on refuting such teaching and affirming that the human soul remains sleeping in the tomb until the Lord returns to earth at the end of the years. times to judge the lost and take his church with him, as we read in Revelation:

"But the other dead did not live again, until the thousand years were over. This is the first resurrection. Blessed and holy is he who has a part in the first resurrection; the second death has no power over these; but they will be priests of God and of Christ, and will reign with him a thousand years." **Revelation 20: 5,6**

"And I saw the dead, great and small, who were before God, and the books were opened; and another book was opened, which is the book of life. And the dead were judged by the things that were written in the books, according to their works.

And the sea gave the dead that were in it; and death and hell gave the dead that were in them; and each was judged according to his works. And death and hell were cast into the lake of fire. This is the second death. And the one who was not found written in the book of life was thrown into the lake of fire". **Revelation 20: 12-15**

This biblical context is the foundation of Christian theology, defending the thesis that we sleep after physical death.

And will only wake up at the Last Judgment, when Christ comes to separate the saved from the lost, the justified from the unbelievers, and those who will reign forever with him , in his Kingdom, of those who will be thrown into the lake of fire together with Satan.

4 - Nobody remembers those who lived in antiquity, and those who are yet to come will not be remembered by those who come after them…

This position may well be contested if we think of the impossibility of remembering our closest relatives and friends, however, this is not the case in particular. What Solomon meant is that we only remember those we know, love or have some affinity with, blood ties and a long relationship. Others, however, that we never had contact or even lived with on a daily basis, however he was not an interesting, expressive person, he had no purchasing power, he was poor, with no future, we didn't even have any memories after his death.

This can happen even with members of our families who are in an economic condition inferior to ours, a neighbor, a co-worker ... Unfortunately, we human beings tend to only value those people that we consider important, whether in our life or on TV. A star of music, cinema or of a highly expressive social pattern when dying is reported in the media and this is recorded in our memories. John Lennon died in 1980, murdered by a fan. Michael Jackson passed away on June 25 in the year 2009 of cardiac arrest, several other stars, politicians, singers, actresses and actors lost their lives decades ago and we still member, but a neighbor who died last week has forgotten. For that is exactly what the sage wanted to express in his words, the simplest we forget most easily, we will never remember them again.

Human Life and Its Consequences

Remember also your Creator in the days of your youth, before the bad days come, and the years come when you will say: I am not content with them.

Before the sun, and the light, and the moon, and the stars are darkened, and the clouds come again after the rain.

On the day when the guards of the house tremble, and the strong men bow down, and the grinders cease, because they are few, and those who look out the windows are darkened.

And the doors of the street are closed because of the low noise of the grinding, and to rise to the voice of the birds, and all the daughters of the music are downed.

As also when they fear that which is high, and there are frights on the way, and the almond tree blooms, and the locust is a burden, and the appetite perishes; because the man goes to his eternal house, and the mourners will walk around the square.

Before the silver cord is broken, and the golden cup is broken, and the pitcher by the fountain is broken, and the wheel by the well is broken. And the dust will return to the earth, as it were, and the spirit will return to God, who gave it." **Ecclesiastes 12: 1-7**

1 - Remember your Creator in the days of your youth ...

It is common for young people to show no interest in approaching God as long as they have the strength and energy to serve him in the preaching of the Gospel, leaving this mission in their lives for when they are older. But, it is a tremendous mistake to think that we should only approach him when old age and the day of our death approach in the idea that the Lord is just a door to enter heaven.

Here, Solomon continues to rebuke young people for several generations and warns them that joining Christ in his important mission to save sinners only after losing physical strength, the strength of vision and mind is an enormous lack of wisdom, because , when this has happened they will be of no use in this important redemptive work.

The entire biblical text we read in Ecclesiastes 12: 1-7 speaks exclusively on this topic. God expects the young people of his people to be ready to go into battle against evil now, while his forces have not yet abandoned them and are useful in getting out. around the world, through hills, hills, countries, cities, alleys and ditches, announcing that the Lord's mercy is still available to all who wish to live in heavenly mansions. The army of Jesus Christ on earth is large, but not everyone is willing to roll up their shirtsleeves and fight for the faith and salvation of sinners; most of them sit by the side of the road, just looking at those who advance.

The Vanity of Human Life

How many of us were vain during our youth and because of that we made countless mistakes? I believe that we all act in the same way, especially those who are born in this generation where freedom is allowed in all ways and the laws that should put a brake on youthful riot support their irresponsible attitudes.

In the last century, young people smoked marijuana, practiced free sex, sometimes gathered in packs and fought in the streets ... But the vast majority studied, respected their parents and were repressed by the police who had the authority to arrest, beat, punish more offenders. Today, our authorities created laws that weakened the police's power of action, teenagers were given the freedom to steal, kill, cause rebellions, panic in the streets of our cities, use heavy drugs like crack, snort cocaine, traffic, without any penalty.

Nowadays these child criminals do what they want, they force good people to live in fear, locked behind bars in their homes while these criminals walk freely in the streets and, when they take the life of a family man or a good citizen , are taken to the presence of a psychologist to receive advice as if these vagabonds take advice into account, because if so they would hear their parents. If the world celebrates technological and scientific developments in the social sphere, we are delayed.

On this topic, we read:

"Rejoice, young man, in your youth, and let your heart be refreshed in the days of your youth, and walk in the ways of your heart, and in the sight of your eyes; know, however, that for all these things God will bring you to judgment. So turn away the wrath from your heart, and remove evil from your flesh, because adolescence and youth are vanity. "**Ecclesiastes 11: 9,10**

According to the words of the sage, one day we will give an account of all our acts practiced during our youth and I can affirm to the reader that this is an indisputable truth, because at fifty-five years of age I was able to experience the bitter taste of God's demands for mistakes made in the past.

For example, if during our youth we were rude and responsive to our parents when we reached maturity and formed our families, we will generate children of similar attitudes, if we get involved with homosexuals or defend the LGBT cause we can have gay children in our home.

 If we were extravagant or addictions like alcohol and tobacco there is a great possibility that one of our heirs will receive this damned inheritance, if we frequent prostitutes we may have this problem mirrored in a son or daughter.

It may seem silly, a pointless idea, but you can believe it because it is true. The biblical statement that we will reap everything we plant is the purest truth and God will not charge us for our mistakes while we are still young because he knows that we are not mature enough to understand his demands, however, after reaching maturity we will have wisdom to discern the right or wrong

The Importance of Good Seed

C*ast your bread on the water, because after many days you will find it. Share with seven, and even eight, because you don't know what harm will be done on the earth.*

When the clouds are full, they pour rain on the earth, and the tree falls to the south, or to the north, in the place where the tree falls there.

Whoever watches the wind will never sow, and whoever looks at the clouds will never reap.

Just as you do not know the path of the wind, nor how the bones are formed in the womb of the pregnant woman, so you do not know the works of God, who does all things.

In the morning sow your seed, and in the afternoon do not remove your hand, because you do not know which one will thrive, if this hand, if that one, or if both will be equally good. " **Ecclesiastes 11: 1-6**

1 - Cast your bread on the water ...

This is an extremely useful recommendation for all those who may want to guarantee the best for the future. In his extreme wisdom Solomon was inspired by the Lord to guide us on the need to throw our bread (to share our goods) on the earth while we live so that in the future we will reap good results.

Most people, especially the most economically affluent, tend to live with their noses high and not caring about the needs of others, believing that they will never fall into misfortune. However, we know several cases of millionaire people who after a while lost everything and were in complete misery. A short time ago I was able to witness in the media the story of a man who won sixty million reais in the

Lotteries and instead of helping the family he abandoned his wife, children and mother, going to live in a penthouse in one of the most luxurious hotels in the city from Recife, in the capital of Pernambuco, and for five years snubbed lust, spending all his money on the most expensive prostitutes.

Later he became completely poor and had to leave the hotel because he was unable to pay the daily absurdities. He did not invest the money he earned, he did not renovate his mother's house, and now he lives there in the old woman's hut that has nothing in the fridge, except water, and live working in a warehouse, carrying boxes on her head, earning a monthly salary a month. .

I worked in a company for thirty-one years and witnessed another degrading scene there. My former boss, because he thought he was too rich, brought us together one day in the auditorium and said he would be firing all the employees and passing the company on to the manager who would choose who he would continue to work with from now on.

The same would receive the company and all of us to work for a year in the place, everything that he earned would be his as a form of indemnity for his more than forty years of services rendered. Then he would return the company to the boss and should follow his course with all of us.

In just nine months, our new boss had already bought land in a privileged location, his new firm was built and we moved there. Years later we saw the former businessman sitting in front of the ex-employee, asking him for a loan to start a new company, as he lost everything he had and wanted to start over.

These two examples show us how important it is to know how to manage our goods and sow our seeds wisely. That man received the help he needed because he wisely invested in his employee, who out of gratitude extended his hand to him at a time when he was at his worst, it was as if he had made a long-term savings and could make a living from there.

2 - Whoever watches the wind will never sow, and whoever looks at the clouds will never reap ...

This quote by the author of Ecclesiastes emphasizes the sad situation of lazy people, as they will never make progress in their mean, still lives, without wanting to make any effort. These people live in inertia, with their mouths open, waiting for someone to sympathize with them and put food between their teeth. We can find these kinds of people everywhere, even family members.

One of the wisest things to do in these cases is to turn your back on such individuals and let them be forced to fight for their own livelihood, since feeding their parasitism will only make them remain exclusively dependent on others. No matter who they are, whether family members or strangers, let them wake up and realize that life is not easy.

3 - We do not understand the works of God ...

How many times do we murmur because we immediately understand the action of God in our lives.

But that is only because of our imperfection we are unable to understand the reasons that lead him to allow certain things. I want to quote again the words of the Lord that were spoken by the prophet's mouth to Israel:

"Porque os meus pensamentos não são os vossos pensamentos, nem os vossos caminhos os meus caminhos, diz o Senhor. Porque assim como os céus são mais altos do que a terra, assim são os meus caminhos mais altos do que os vossos caminhos, e os meus pensamentos mais altos do que os vossos pensamentos." **Isaías 55:8,9**.

"Não temas, porque eu sou contigo; não te assombres, porque eu sou teu Deus; eu te fortaleço, e te ajudo, e te sustento com a destra da minha justiça. Eis que, envergonhados e confundidos serão todos os que se indignaram contra ti; tornar-se-ão em nada, e os que contenderem contigo, perecerão.

Buscá-los-ás, porém não os acharás; os que pelejarem contigo, tornar-se-ão em nada, e como coisa que não é nada, os que guerrearem contigo. Porque eu, o Senhor teu Deus, te tomo pela tua mão direita; e te digo: Não temas, eu te ajudo." **Isaías 41:10-13**

The Infinite Knowledge of God

The Lord has a deep and infinite knowledge of all things, including each of his creatures and his children, which goes from his birth to the day of his death. Aware of this was that David wrote Psalm 139, confessing that only God was to know its beginning, middle and end. The human being is born, grows and dies without first having a relative perspective on how he will leave this world, no matter how he guesses the final answer always comes from his Creator.

At least three years ago I lost a blood brother to a serious car accident, when in fact he lives in a critical state of diabetes and had already lost the two kidneys that stopped working and needed to undergo hemodialysis constantly. All of us, relatives, believed that his departure would happen through the disease, however, he died in that tragic accident. As King David said, only he knows our day.

"Lord, you have searched me, and you know me. You know my settling and my raising; you understand my thoughts from afar. You surround my walk, and my bed; and you know all my ways. There being no word yet in my language, behold, O Lord, you know everything at once. You surrounded me from behind and ahead, and laid your hand on me. Such science is wonderful to me; so high that I can't reach it.

Where will I go from your spirit, or where will I flee from your face? If you go up to heaven, there you are; if I make my bed in hell, behold, you are there too.

If you take the wings of the morning, if you live at the ends of the sea, your hand will guide me there, and your right hand will sustain me. If I say: Surely the darkness will cover me; then the night will be light around me.

Even darkness does not cover me from you; but the night shines like the day; darkness and light are the same to you.

For you have possessed my kidneys; you covered me in my mother's womb.

I will praise you, because in an amazing and so wonderful way I was made; Your works are wonderful, and my soul knows it very well.

My bones were not hidden from you, when in the occult I was made, and woven into the depths of the earth.

Your eyes have seen my body still shapeless; and in your book all these things were written; which in continuation were formed, when there was not even one of them.

And how precious your thoughts are to me, O God! How big are their sums! If I counted them, they would be more than sand; when i wake up i'm still with you. O God, you will surely kill the wicked; therefore depart from me, men of blood. For they speak evil against you; and your enemies take your name in vain. Do I not hate those who hate you, o Lord, and do I not grieve for those who rise up against you? I hate them with perfect hatred; I have them for enemies. Search me.

O God, and know my heart; prove me, and know my thoughts. And see if there is any evil path in me, and guide me on the eternal path. Psalm 139: 1-24

Let us do like David, a man who was praised by God for the size of his loyalty, faith, dedication and faithfulness. Let us ask him to search our hearts and make us aware of our bad ways. Let us cry out for his mercy so that he can forgive us and turn our evil into works of justice, because only he knows us deeply and can fix our imperfections.

"Have mercy on me, O God, according to your lovingkindness; erase my transgressions, according to the multitude of your mercies.

Wash me completely from my iniquity, and cleanse me from my sin.

Because I know my transgressions, and my sin is always before me.

Against you, against you, I have only sinned, and done what is evil in your sight, so that you will be justified when you speak, and pure when you judge.

Behold, in iniquity I was formed, and in sin my mother conceived me.

Behold, you love the truth within, and in the hidden you make me know wisdom. Purify me with hyssop, and I will be pure; wash me, and I will be whiter than snow.

Make me hear joy and joy, so that the bones you have broken will enjoy.

Hide your face from my sins, and erase all my iniquities.

Create in me a clean heart, O God, and renew a right spirit in me.

Do not cast me out of your presence, and do not take your Holy Spirit from me.

Give me the joy of your salvation again, and support me with a willing spirit. Then I will teach transgressors your ways, and sinners will be converted to you.

Deliver me from blood crimes, O God, God of my salvation, and my tongue will highly praise your righteousness.

Open my lips, Lord, and my mouth will sing your praise.

For you do not desire sacrifices, otherwise I would give them; you do not delight in burnt offerings. Sacrifices for God are the broken spirit; You will not despise a broken and contrite heart, O God.

Do good to Zion, according to your good will; build the walls of Jerusalem. Then you will be pleased with the sacrifices of justice, the burnt offerings and the burnt offerings; then bulls will be offered on your altar.

Psalm 51: 1-1

Bible Quotes

Isaiah 53: 4

[4] Truly he took our infirmities upon himself, and our pains he took upon himself and we regarded him as afflicted, wounded by God, and oppressed.

Are Your Faith and Love growing?

I will improve my question: Are your Faith in God and your love for your brothers growing?

Yeah, the situation is kind of complicated with this virus, isn't it? What have you been thinking about it?

I want to bring you a little more calm in this moment of crisis.

Isaiah 53 says that Jesus took our pains and OUR ENDINGS!

Psalm 91 assures us that:

Guarded by the Lord we would not be affected!

Jesus called Peter to walk on water and while he was focused on God he walked on water and lived the supernatural, but when he focused on the storm he started to sink. Our focus defines what we are experiencing.

In times of crisis we need to remember what brings us hope. We need to be with a divine mentality and keep the Word in our hearts, memorizing biblical passages is sometimes complicated, isn't it?

Don't let bad experiences limit what the Word says. It tells us that the Lord not only heals, but HE IS THE HEAL FOR ALL OUR EVIL.

Elevate your experiences to biblical truths, like the truth that Jesus says we would do even greater works than He did among men. If He healed, we can also pray and bring healing to the sick in His name.

We already have the solution that the World needs in the Word and the more biblical texts you have on the tip of your tongue, the more you will be grounded in memorizing it.

The Word of God contained in the Holy Bible is the way to face all situations and if we are grounded in it, we need not fear any harm. AND DON'T FORGET:

The Bible predicts all these events, and it is not because we are children that we can be inconsequential, but we need to trust that the Lord is our strength and very present help in distress. We need to have faith.

Luke 14: 11

[11] For whoever exalts himself will be humbled, and whoever humbles himself will be exalted.

Every time you exalt yourself, you fall.

And I am one hundred percent sure when I say this, first, because it is in the Bible: "Pride precedes destruction; arrogance precedes the fall" (Proverbs. 16:18) and, second: We all need Jesus not to stumble over our mistakes. So whenever we are filled with self-confidence with the arrogance of someone who is not susceptible to error, we fall. We fall because we trust too much in our sinful nature, we trust too much in the strength of our own arm. And it says a lot about where our heart really is.

To walk with Jesus is to learn about humility, it is to be humble to recognize how flawed we are, how much we have made mistakes and are constantly changing.

Many men in the Bible have become self-confident and have forgotten that we have no strength in the face of an Almighty God who can do all things.

Azarias, Nebuchadnezzar and Herod Agrippa were among them. Arrogance preceded the ruin of these men and may precede ours as well.

We are nothing compared to who God is.

Never be filled with exaggerated confidence because of your knowledge, your training or even the intimacy you say you have with God.

You are susceptible to error, we always are and it takes courage to recognize that. There is nothing wrong with being the right person, doing things the right way and trying to be dedicated in everything we do, but we will not always get it right, let us recognize it!

And, most of all, whenever we make mistakes, we run at the Lord's feet just as David did. We tear ourselves up before the presence of God and do not allow our mistakes to define who we are.

John 16:33

"In the world you will have afflictions, but be of good cheer; I won the world "

We don't know when, but at any moment we can go through a storm. Real problems!

It is not possible to say what kind of problems will appear. Perhaps a debilitating illness or suddenly, a life threatening illness. Perhaps the loss of someone we love. Perhaps the burden of poverty, the shedding of blood, whatever it may be, I repeat: Jesus himself said: "In this world they will have afflictions" (Jn 16.33 NIV).

Jesus said these words in the Upper Room of the Temple, when sharing his Last Supper with his disciples. He knew that his hour had come and that he would soon suffer for the sins of the world. As he foresaw the time when he would no longer be there, he knew that his disciples would face one problem after another, and indeed the persecutions were great after that.

This theme appears repeatedly in his final speeches. Jesus told the disciples that he would soon leave them (John 13: 33, 36; 16: 28). I told them that the world would hate them as much as it hated Him (John 15: 18–19). I told them that people would try to kill them (John 16: 2) and that they would cry and lament in sadness and anguish (John 16: 20). I told them that they would abandon him and spread everywhere (John 16: 32).

Finally, he summed up all his tribulations in the simple statement: "In this world you will have afflictions". Although these words were spoken specifically to the first disciples, they remain relevant today for anyone who wants to make a difference in the world through Jesus Christ. One thing is certain: Problems will always be on the way.

It is the normal experience of God's suffering people in this sinful world. What Jesus said to the disciples has been true for his church throughout the centuries: "In this world you will have afflictions". But He also said, "I will be with you every day, until the end of the age." So, cheer up, we are all more than winners in the one who called us.

John 16:33

"I have told you this, that you may have peace in me; in the world you will have afflictions, but, be of good cheer, I have overcome the world. "

I won the world.

What may seem strange about this promise is the tense used by Jesus. Remember that he said those words the night before he died on the cross. Jesus had not yet accomplished the work for which he came into the world. However, he stated: "I have overcome the world!"

As far as Jesus is concerned, the work of our salvation was as if it had already been done. He had already resisted every temptation to sin. He was therefore fully prepared to offer his life in perfect sacrifice.

The historical events that would take him to the cross, to the tomb and then out of it had already begun. By faith, Jesus was looking forward to the day when his promise would be fulfilled, the moment when he would conquer the world.

What does this promise mean to us today?

If Jesus overcame the world, then death was defeated, the debt of sin was canceled and the door to eternal life is already open. Therefore, our problems are only temporary, and any suffering we experience will never separate us from the love of God because we are in Jesus Christ.

If Christ overcame the world, we can overcome it too. We can resist temptation. We can persevere in the midst of persecution. We can live for Christ and his Kingdom. We can also die for him, having full hope of receiving all his promises.

1 Samuel 12:23

"And as for me, far be it from me that I sin against the Lord, stopping praying for you: first I will teach you the good and right way."

In II Tm. 2: 1, The Lord invites us to pray for all men. Caring for each other in prayer is one of the most beautiful ways to show love, because it is the purest love that exists, prayer should be without any interest. Some feel that intercession is a ministry to an exclusive group in the church and are mistaken, as this is the duty of every Christian.

In fact, it is this "select group" that I want to talk about today. Yes, the famous "Sisters of the Prayer Circle".

A few years ago, when someone needed answers from Heaven, it was normal to go to churches to look for sisters or prayer groups. Today I still see it happening, but it is not as common as it once was.

People who were desperate and aimlessly went to churches seeking to talk to people connected with God in prayer. Unfortunately, people took advantage of this and some things became commonplace. Lack of fear when delivering a word, saying that God is speaking when he is not, laying on of hands and false revelations are some examples.

Moreover, even though some were irresponsible, God continues to work through people, after all, it was never about us, and not even about what we can do, it is all for Him. Through Him and for Him.

We can claim that He can work through our lives. Have you ever thought of praying for a sick person and him being healed? People asking for your help in seeking an answer from God? None of this is for his name, but for his name to be glorified.

God's intention is for us to be one with Him and with our brothers to experience perfect unity. Let us be aware that there are many gifts available and that if we ask God, He will gladly give us, just let Him use us.

There is something special within us that has been given to us by God and needs to go out to reach other people.

Let us move in a supernatural way, intensify our relationship with God and experience things never imagined possible.

Let us renounce the "we are not able" syndrome. In fact, we will never achieve anything alone, but it is Christ who lives in us and He can do all things.

Romans 8:32

"He who spared not even his own Son, but gave him up for us all, how can he not also give us all things with him?"

The most comprehensive promise of God's grace is found in Rom. 8:32. This is surely the most precious verse in the Bible. Part of the reason is that the promise in it is so complete that it can help us with just about every turn in our life and ministry. There has never been and never will be a circumstance in our lives when that promise is irrelevant.

This all-encompassing promise alone would probably not make this verse the most precious. There are other great and similar promises like Sl. 84: 11: "No good [God] evades those who walk uprightly". E 1 Co 3: 21-23: "Everything is yours: Be it Paul, be Apollo, be Cephas, be the world, be life, be death, be things present, be things to come, be yours, and you, of Christ, and Christ, of God ". It is difficult to overstate the spectacular scope and scope of these promises.

However, what puts Rm. 8:32 in a class alone is the logic that gives rise to the promise and makes it as solid and unshakable as God's love for his infinitely admirable Son.

Rom. 8:32 contains a foundation and a guarantee that are so strong, solid, and sure that there is absolutely no possibility of this promise being broken.

This makes it an ever-present force in times of great distress. No matter what changes, whatever disappoint, whatever else fails, that comprehensive promise of grace will never fail.

"He who did not spare his own Son, before, for all of us gave him ...".

If that is true, says the logic of heaven, then God will surely give all things to those to whom he gave his Son!

Psalm 100: 4

"Enter through his doors with praise, and into his courts with hymns: praise him and bless his name."

Every time in the presence of God is always a moment of praise. When we are in church, at work or even at home, whenever we are communicating with God, be grateful. Let us remember all the good things he has done for us in our lives and give him due praise.

The Bible says that He dwells in the midst of praises, at any time, even in the most difficult, even if it is not easy, let us praise the Lord.

Think of the disciples spending time with Jesus on a boat when a menacing storm breaks out in the sea. They were unprepared to face her and, in a panic, realize that they may die. All the while Jesus was sleeping soundly.

Instead of looking at the Master's reaction to their critical situation, the disciples allowed fear to dictate how they would react.

After begging Jesus to do something, He calms the storm... But not before asking them, "Why are you so afraid? His slight rebuke of their lack of faith was not because they did not believe that he could save them from the storm, but because they had difficulty believing that He would be interested in helping them at that time. When we are overwhelmed by life we always have two choices:

Focus on your circumstances or fix your eyes on Jesus. If we choose to look at Jesus above anything, we will begin to see that the storms faced are nowhere near as powerful as we think, if the Savior chooses to weather the storm at our side. So let's hold your hands and move on.

Matthew 26: 37

"And taking Peter and the two sons of Zebedee with him, he began to be saddened and very distressed."

There were six ways in which Jesus fought depression, there were several tactics in Jesus' strategic battle against discouragement.

1- He chose some close friends to be with Him.

"Taking Peter and the two sons of Zebedee with him" (Mt. 26: 37).

2- He opened his soul to them. He told them:

"My soul is deeply sad until death" (Mt. 26: 38).

3- He asked for your intercession and companionship in battle.

"Stay here and watch with me" (Mt. 26: 38).

4- He poured out his heart to the Father in prayer.

"My Father, if possible, pass this cup on me!" (Mt. 26: 39).

5- He rested his soul in the sovereign wisdom of God.

"However, do not be as I want but as you want" (Mt. 26: 39).

6- He fixed his gaze on the glorious future blessing that awaited him on the other side of the cross.

"In exchange for the joy that was proposed to him, [he] endured the cross, ignoring ignominy and is seated at the right hand of the throne of God" (Heb. 12: 2).

When something happens in your life that seems to threaten your future, remember this: The first oscillations of the bomb are not the effects of sin in your life, the real danger is giving in to them, giving yourself in, not starting any spiritual struggle.

And the root of that surrender is unbelief. Failure to fight for faith in future victory, failure to appreciate everything God promises to be for us in Christ.

Jesus shows us another way, not without pain or passive, follow him, find your spiritual and trustworthy friends, open your soul to them, ask them to watch and pray with you, pour your soul to the Father, rest in the sovereign wisdom of God and fix your eyes on the joy that is before you, on the precious and magnificent promises of God.

1 John 3:18

"My little children, let us not love in word, nor in tongue, but in deed and in truth."

The truest way to express the love we profess is through our actions. Our actions are a reflection of our thoughts and what we keep in our hearts.

Think about your actions. Do they speak of true love or are they contrary to the pure love of God? We need to reflect the love that resides in our hearts and in all our actions. Let us not be hypocrites, claiming to love, but, in fact, demonstrating the opposite. Let us ask the Lord to enable us to truly love.

Let us do this, for we ourselves have no capacity to love as our God, since love is suffering; he is benign, he is not jealous, he does not treat lightly, he does not puff up, he does not behave indecently, he does not seek his interests, he does not get angry, he does not suspect evil; do not take leave with injustice, but take leave with truth, everything suffers, everything believes, everything hopes, everything endures. (1 Co. 13: 4-7).

Christ warns us to love even those who hate us:

"But I say to you, love your enemies, bless those who curse you, do good to those who hate you. Pray for those who mistreat you and persecute you; (Mt. 5: 44),

For He who does not love does not know God, since God is love. **(1 John 4: 8).**

Exodus 34: 2

"And prepare for tomorrow, so that you can go up in the morning to Mount Sinai, and there stand before me, on the top of the mountain."

The story of Moses receiving the Ten Commandments at Mount Sinai is among the most famous in the Bible. Moses is alone with God for forty days at the top of the mountain. In the end, he descends with two stone planks and his face is radiant. We do not know much about this mysterious period of isolation other than the fact that Moses was *"without eating bread and without drinking water"* **(Ex. 34: 28).** When we consult the book of Deuteronomy, we have an additional detail:

"And I fell down before the Lord, those forty days and forty nights when I was prostrate, because the Lord had said that He wanted to destroy you." **(Deut. 9: 25)**

The original Hebrew term for "to be prostrate" is ethnapal, from the root N-P-L ("to fall"). This is an extremely rare word in the Bible, which literally means "I threw myself down." This unique Hebrew word is the key to understanding Moses' spiritual character.

We need to strengthen our connection with the Lord and His Word. As we read the Bible we understand that Moses was not merely lying on the floor waiting for the forty days to end. Instead, he actively engaged in prayer and fasting to atone for the sins of the people.

Acts 28: 31

"Preaching the kingdom of God, and teaching, with all freedom, the things belonging to the Lord Jesus Christ, without any impediment."

While Paul was a prisoner in Rome, he still needed to preach and teach. He did it with confidence and no one told him to stop. It is interesting that even while he was a prisoner, he managed to spread the Gospel.

Paul was imprisoned, but instead of revolting and holding on to self-pity or despair he recognized that he could still glorify God despite that situation. At times our present condition can seem bleak because God allows such events to happen to us. So, we can glorify God in all situations or simply murmur.

There is no situation that you face in which God cannot be glorified. Wherever you are, no matter how difficult the circumstance, seek to glorify him.

We don't always like the situations we find ourselves in. Life is sometimes difficult and seems unfair. And we find ourselves, at times, overwhelmed. On other occasions, alone. At these times we must ask the Lord to help us to glorify Him in any situation in which we may find ourselves. God is sovereign and is in control of all things. We can have peace in knowing that He holds the world in His hands.

Who knows everything about us. If we trust him in the most difficult situations, Jesus will surely give us victory.

Hebrews 3: 13

"Rather, exhort one another, every day, during the time that is called Today, so that none of you may be hardened by the deceit of sin"

To exhort another believer is to encourage him in truth and to correct him with love. If we do not love our brothers and sisters in Christ enough to correct and encourage them, then they can sin for so long that their hearts will be hardened.

They can stop avoiding the sin they are committing and continue to sin without thinking about the consequences. Let us be courageous enough to exhort our brothers.

So too, when we are reprimanded, we need to be humble to accept correction. Only God helps us to thank and listen to his exhortation.

He gives us courage and grace to correct others properly, as well as to accept constructive guidance. We must do it only with love, not diminishing our brothers. Exhortation softens the hearts and reveals the evil in us.

Let us pray that the Lord will give us eyes to see our sins and hearts to turn away from our perverse ways and get closer to Jesus.

Isaiah 6: 5

"Then I said: Woe is me, I am perishing! Because I am a man of unclean lips and I live in the midst of a people of unclean lips and my eyes have seen the king, the Lord of hosts! '

Having this vision and seeing how holy God is, Isaiah panicked, he felt unworthy. He was sinful and dirty compared to the greatness of God. He lived and lived among other equally sinful human beings.

Have you ever experienced a similar sensation? God is so good, we are the ones who are covered by the dirt of sin. The Lord is holy, just, perfect, worthy, eternal and no one can fit Him. Isaiah was concerned about his filthy state. What could he do? How could I endure such a perfect and infinitely powerful God? We see in the next two verses that God has purified him.

Recognizing that we are not worthy to remain in his presence, we are not worthy to untie his shoes or wash his feet, for God is indescribably good and we are nothing compared to his glory. We are proud to think that things revolve around us, that we are important and incredible. But we are nothing, only God is truly incredible.

We are disobedient. We are unable to observe its precepts, we are rebellious and disobedient. Therefore, let us confess our weaknesses and trust the Lord as Isaiah did, He will cleanse us.

Ephesians 4: 15

"Rather, following the truth in love, let us grow, in everything, in the one who is the head, Christ."

This part of the scripture describes believers maturing and growing in Christ. She talks about believers being like children in maturity, but then gives instructions on how to grow in Christ. One of those things is how to speak the truth in love.

It is difficult to speak the truth in love. We don't want to hurt and disappoint people, so we are afraid to tell them something. Other times, we fear your anger. Sometimes we speak the truth out of selfishness and not out of love.

When we see something wrong in the lives of other believers, we can tell them the truth. However, we must not do it in anger, we must do it because of the love we have for God and our brothers.

In many cases it takes patience, only the Father in Heaven to give us the necessary serenity with speaking. He will help us to love others. So we must ask him to guide us in the correct way of acting. Love them as He loved and forgave us. Asking him to grant us wisdom on how to speak the truth when others go astray. To give us the words to express ourselves, guided by the Holy Spirit.

Final Considerations

As I finish this work more, I feel grateful to God for the wisdom I have been given to share this knowledge with each of my readers around the world, wherever this book is acquired and read. I dedicate myself more and more to each new work to offer everyone something more valuable and profitable, which can considerably increase the understanding of each student of the Holy Scriptures. Therefore, I leave here my most sincere thanks to those who lovingly accompany me on this mission to comment on the Divine Word and try to explain its mysteries.

Bibliography

— Pentecostal Study Bible, Thompson, New Life, New International Version, King James Version

— Collaboration: Pr. Antônio Carlos Guimarães Baia - President of the Ministry Christ for the Nations - Pages 103 to 127

.

Lightning Source UK Ltd.
Milton Keynes UK
UKRC022302280720
367331UK00005B/130